Understanding Drug Issues

Companion volume

Understanding Drugs
A Handbook for Parents, Teachers and Other Professionals
David Emmett and Graeme Nice
ISBN 1 85302 400 7

of related interest

Challenging Ourselves
Towards Gender Equity and Violence-Free Relationships
A Handbook of Practical Activities
The Metropolitan Toronto School Board
ISBN 1 85302 445 7

Parenting Teenagers
Bob Myers
ISBN 1 85302 366 3

Raising Responsible Teenagers
Bob Myers
ISBN 1 85302 429 5

Project-Based Group Work Facilitator's Manual
Young People, Youth Workers and Projects
Andy Gibson and Gaynor Clarke
ISBN 1 85302 169 5

Group Work with Children and Adolescents
A Handbook
Edited by Kedar Nath Dwivedi
ISBN 1 85302 157 1

Arts Approaches to Conflict
Edited by Marian Liebmann
ISBN 1 85302 293 4

Understanding Drug Issues
A Workbook of Photocopiable Resources
Raising Issues for Young People

Jessica Kingsley Publishers
London and Philadelphia

First published in the United Kingdom in 1998 by
Jessica Kingsley Publishers Ltd
116 Pentonville Road
London N1 9JB, England
and
325 Chestnut Street,
Philadelphia, PA 19106, USA.

www.jkp.com

Second impression 2000

Library of Congress Cataloging in Publication Data
A CIP catalogue record for this book is available from the Library of Congress

British Library Cataloguing in Publication Data
A CIP catalogue record for this book is available from the British Library

Printed and Bound in Great Britain by
Athenaeum Press, Gateshead, Tyne and Wear

Contents

With special thanks to Jean Emmett

and Alan 'Deano' Dent

Acknowledgements

The authors and publishers would like to acknowledge the generosity of GST Technology Ltd and Lotus smartpics for permitting the use of their graphic images.

Introduction

The two of us have been heavily involved in presenting drugs education to young people over many years, and when doing so make it clear that we are not there to tell them 'Don't take drugs.' We would rather that they remained free of street drugs, for our experience in all aspects of this has taught us that for many of them not to do so would be a grave mistake. It is not for us to tell them what to think or what to decide. It is for each young person to do that for themselves. If we were to simply tell them not to do a certain thing, then all they have to do is to reject us, if they choose to do the opposite. If, on the other hand, we enable them to gain knowledge and greater understanding of many of the issues concerning drug use, they then have to reject all of that knowledge and understanding if they still want to get involved: a much more difficult task.

Over the past 20 or so years the style of drugs education presented to our young people has gone through many changes. Our early attempts at drug misuse prevention education depended very largely on the principle of 'shock horror'. Films were produced showing dead and dying drug 'addicts', festering injection sites, and even shots of the post mortem examination of dead users. The simple idea was that scenes of such horror could not fail to put young people off, and that this approach would solve the problem. It soon became clear that the approach was failing, and its effects were very short-lived. Young people were indeed shocked and horrified, but they were also fascinated. The many research projects carried out at the time showed that at best its deterrent effects did not last, and that in some cases it actually encouraged experimentation. This is perhaps not surprising, as most young people believe themselves to be immortal and that such awful things will not happen to them.

Drug prevention education then moved to use of the information model. The simple idea was that if teachers taught young people all about drugs, then they would be able to make the right decisions. The flaw in this approach was that, despite giving them all the facts necessary to make a decision, we failed to teach them how to handle the decision-making process itself. Efforts were then made to deal with this flaw by adopting the 'just say no' approach. Fiercely negative messages were added to the facts so that young people were left only with the choice of accepting the 'just say no' message or rejecting all that they had been taught.

Clearly, with the rapid escalation in young peoples' drug use over the last decade, this approach has also failed to a large extent.

New strategies must therefore be found and utilised whereby young people themselves can be involved in their own education and their views sought and valued. They should be given credit for their own intelligence and insight, and for the power that they hold as potential influencers of their peers.

In this workbook the exercises have been devised not to put young people down by telling them that they are wrong, bad or stupid if they use drugs, but to challenge and inform them. The exercises allow participants to explore their knowledge, attitudes and beliefs about today's drug culture, encouraging them to look at the subject in a less insular manner and to consider a whole range of possibilities. They will be able to reason and decide for themselves how they feel about the many issues raised.

In this way these exercises may encourage them to make informed judgments and decisions about where they fit in around drug use. It is our hope that by treating them in a responsible, respectful and more adult way, they may then make better informed decisions as to their own actions, and by doing so may reduce both the level of drug use and the degree of harm that such use is causing.

The exercises in this workbook take account of many learning styles, and, for that matter, teaching styles too; and we hope that they will cater for the majority rather than the few. It is our intention that these exercises will stimulate young people, and, through raising their awareness, reduce the numbers who may go on to experiment with substances, and those who may go on to develop greater problems through prolonged usage.

EXERCISE 1

What If ?

Suggested age: 13 +

Outline

This exercise allows participants to accept responsibility for preparing advice to the government, which is considering legalising the supply and use of drugs. Participants will have an opportunity to consider the advantages and disadvantages of such action. Suggested length of exercise: one hour.

Purpose and expected outcomes

- To increase awareness of how drugs affect society.
- To increase the participants' sense of community responsibility.
- To encourage individual responsibility over drug decisions.
- To see personal drug use in a wider context.
- To challenge attitudes to drug use.
- To reinforce drug prevention messages.

Method

The teacher or group leader is to outline the exercise and then form the participants into small groups. Each group is allocated a worksheet that covers a different area of responsibility. With large classes, more than one group may be using copies of the same sheet. Allow time for each group to discuss its sheet fully and to make notes of the points raised. At the end of the allocated time, each group is to report back the results of its discussions. Questions may then be asked by the leader or by other members of the class. The leader can then draw together salient issues that have arisen, and organise a vote to arrive at a majority decision as to whether drug legalisation would be advantageous or detrimental to society.

Notes for teacher or group leader

Participants may raise the issue of the legal use of alcohol, and you may wish to discuss with the class whether alcohol and its social use compares with most patterns of illegal drug use. Unlike alcohol, the controlled, low level and social use of most drugs is very difficult to maintain over any length of time. Most of our common illegal drugs of misuse have effects that are more persistent than alcohol. Excessive use of alcohol would be a more relevant comparison, and society already goes to great lengths to control such use, such as the use of simple breath sampling devices. The use of illegal drugs is much more difficult and expensive to detect.

Participants may wish to set special rules for people in certain positions of responsibility, prohibiting them alone from using drugs. This idea should be resisted, for the same rules should apply to all. There are very few people who do not have some responsibilities for others, so if it is permissible for some people to use drugs then it should be permissible for everyone.

Leaders may wish to use the exercise in modified ways, perhaps specifying only certain illegal drugs, or making the participants look at the issues from the standpoint of different members of society.

Follow-up exercises

1. Collecting media articles concerning drug use incidents and evaluating their effect on society.
2. Essay covering differing aspects of drug use.
3. Further group discussion of issues raised during exercise.

Exercise 1.1

ARMED FORCES

You are a member of a team responsible to the government for the operation of its defence forces.

You have been asked to consider the implications of a proposal to legalise the supply and use of drugs.

You might like to include the following in your considerations:

- Personnel on front line duties, including those in charge of weapons, using mind altering substances.

- The possible effects on military discipline.

- Military security, official secrets and espionage.

- The possible effects on military communications.

- The safety of nuclear and other weapons etc.

- Co-operation and planning with allies.

- The effect on negotiations.

- Safety of personnel, planes, ships, vehicles, etc.

REMEMBER -- CONSIDER ALL POSSIBLE OUTCOMES

Exercise 1.2

HEALTH CARE

You are a member of a team responsible to the government for the provision of health care in your district.

You have been asked to consider the implications of a proposal to legalise the supply and use of drugs.

You might like to include the following in your considerations:

- Hospital staff using mind altering substances.

- The effect on future needs and costs of health care provision (e.g. patient numbers).

- Health issues around injecting drugs.

- Use of substances by surgical staff.

- The physical health of the nation.

- The psychiatric health of the nation.

- Babies born to drug-using parents.

- Use of drugs by family doctors, district nurses, dentists, etc.

REMEMBER – CONSIDER ALL POSSIBLE OUTCOMES

Exercise 1.3

EDUCATION

You are a member of a team responsible to the Government for the provision of education in your district.

You have been asked to consider the implications of a proposal to legalise the supply and use of drugs.

You might like to include the following in your considerations:

- Possible effects on the quality of education.
- Truancy rates of pupils / absenteeism by staff.
- Achievement levels of pupils who use drugs and their effect on non-drug using pupils.

- Possible effects on school discipline.
- Education standards / league tables.
- Academic reputation of the country.
- Possible effects on pupil / teacher relations.
- Safety during practical lessons, physical activities, science experiments and outside visits.

REMEMBER – CONSIDER ALL POSSIBLE OUTCOMES

Exercise 1.4

LAW AND ORDER – PUBLIC SAFETY

You are a member of a team responsible to the government for the provision of community safety and security in your district.

You have been asked to consider the implications of a proposal to legalise the supply and use of drugs.

You might like to include the following in your considerations:

- Police officers/fire fighters using mind altering substances.

- Police/fire response to incidents.

- Possible effects on prison discipline and security.

- Possible effect on street crime.

- Effects on justice, e.g. judges, juries, magistrates or witnesses using drugs.

- Organised crime and terrorism.

- Road safety.

- Effects on public order.

REMEMBER – CONSIDER ALL POSSIBLE OUTCOMES

Exercise 1.5

TOURISM

You are a member of a team responsible to the government for the encouragement of tourism.

You have been asked to consider the implications of a proposal to legalise the supply and use of drugs.

You might like to include the following in your considerations:

- Tourists who come just to buy and use drugs.
- The effect on family tourism to the country.
- The reputation of the country in the eyes of foreign tourists.
- The arrival of foreign dealers to supply drugs.
- The effect on street safety in major tourism areas.

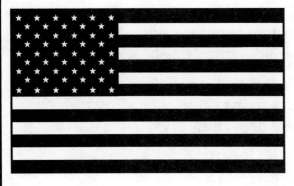

- The effect on the reputation of UK citizens visiting other countries.
- Relationships with other countries where drugs remain illegal and whose citizens visit the UK.

REMEMBER – CONSIDER ALL POSSIBLE OUTCOMES

Exercise 1.6

EMPLOYMENT

You are a member of a team responsible to the government for employment.

You have been asked to consider the implications of a proposal to legalise the supply and use of drugs.

You might like to include the following in your considerations:

- Possible effects on production levels.
- Workers operating dangerous machinery whilst affected by substances.
- Levels of absenteeism and sickness in the work force.
- Relationships between staff and employers.
- Quality of work needing high levels of accuracy carried out by staff using substances.

- Relationships between drug using staff and their non-drug using colleagues.
- Business and trade union leaders affected by mind altering substances whilst making important decisions.

REMEMBER – CONSIDER ALL POSSIBLE OUTCOMES

What a Bargain!

Suggested age: 12+

Outline

This exercise enables participants to explore some of the issues that are associated with buying drugs. Participants will look first at information that they may wish to have before they can make a sensible decision as to whether to purchase a particular car or not. They will then extend that idea to the purchase of illegal drugs, and the information they require before deciding whether to purchase or not. Participants will have an opportunity to assess how important it is to have accurate information when making such purchases, and to express their views regarding doing so without such information. Suggested length of exercise: one hour.

Purpose and expected outcomes

- To improve participants' understanding of drugs.
- To encourage participants to explore drug-related decisions.
- To challenge attitudes to drug use.
- To reinforce drug prevention messages.

Method

The teacher or group leader is to outline the exercise and then form the participants into small groups. Each group is to be issued with the blank worksheet that deals with the purchase of a car (we suggest that this sheet is photocopied to A3 size). The leader will explain that the particpants are to imagine that they have seen a secondhand car and are considering buying it. Each group is then asked to list the information that it needs before deciding whether to buy or not. Time is allowed for group discussion, and each group reports back to the rest of the class on the issues that they have discussed. The leader may need to restrict feedback, so that every group has a chance to contribute. The car check-list can then be used as an OHP slide and compared with the ideas raised by the participants. The various categories of information can then be discussed and placed in order of importance. The blank worksheet that deals with the purchase of an illegal drug is then issued, and each group asked to discuss the information it requires before deciding whether to purchase or not. Time is allowed for discussion, and then each group reports back to the rest of the class on the issues that they have raised. The leader can then use the drug check-list as an OHP slide and compare it with the groups' lists. As with the car purchase, the categories can be discussed and the information placed in order of importance. The class may then be asked to consider where good, accurate information can be obtained on both cars and illegal drugs; and the opinion it would hold of somebody who bought a car without previously finding out as much as possible about it. This can then be compared with the way in which most people buy illegal drugs.

Notes for teacher or group leader

The availability of good, balanced and accurate information regarding drugs is very important. Some users or potential users may consider much of the information that is made available from official sources to be propaganda rather than fact. The leader may obtain supplies of such drugs literature and compare it with information that is available from other bodies working in the drugs field. (See appendix for a list of helping agencies.)

Follow-up exercises

1. Participants can also collect copies of advertisements for different products and study the information given. They can then assess the degree of importance that manufacturers attach to information they believe purchasers want. A comparison can then be made with the degree of information offered to users by those selling illegal drugs.

2. A further comparison can be made by collecting information that is supplied with medical drugs.

WHAT SHOULD YOU ASK BEFORE BUYING A CAR ?

WHAT SHOULD YOU ASK BEFORE BUYING A CAR ?

PRICE & RUNNING COSTS
1. Sale price
2. Affordability
3. Will it hold its value?
4. Servicing costs
5. Tyre costs
6. Petrol consumption
7. Insurance
8. Value for money
9. Guarantee/warranty
10. Repair costs

PERFORMANCE
1. Engine size
2. Speed
3. Acceleration
4. Road holding

LEGALITY
1. Roadworthy?
2. Insurance/tax
3. Stolen?

SAFETY
1. Speed
2. Brakes
3. Road-holding
4. Tyres/steering
5. Body condition/rust
6. Modified?
7. Suitability for use

IMAGE
1. Colour
2. Style
3. Engine size
4. Speed and acceleration
5. Make/age
6. Stereo system
7. Condition
8. Meets your needs?

HISTORY
1. Mileage/users
2. Service history
3. Reputation

WHAT SHOULD YOU ASK BEFORE BUYING A DRUG?

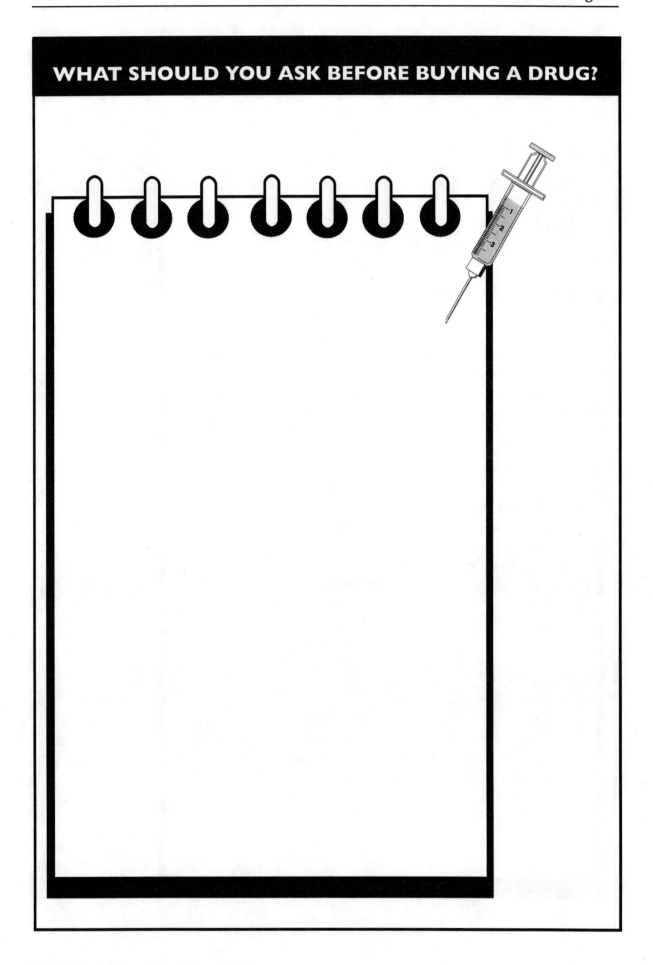

WHAT SHOULD YOU ASK BEFORE BUYING A DRUG?

PRICE AND FUTURE COSTS
1. Sale price
2. Habit forming?
3. Tolerance
4. Withdrawal
5. Side effects
6. Availability
7. Affordability

PERFORMANCE
1. Expected effects
2. Fulfils your needs?
3. Strength/tolerance
4. Method of use
5. Reliability
6. Predictability

LEGALITY
1. Penalties for possession, supply etc.
2. Effects of prosecution on education and future prospects

SAFETY
1. Strength
2. Purity/additives
3. Snideys (false drugs)
4. Tolerance
5. Overdose
6. Withdrawal
7. Side effects
8. Methods of use
9. Reliability
10. Predictability
11. Risks/dangers
12. Unexpected effects

IMAGE
1. Street credibility
2. Fashionable?
3. Reputation
4. Method of use

HISTORY
1. Accurate information available?
2. Reputation/background
3. Known problems

Safety Ladder

Suggested age: 14+

Outline

This exercise is designed to allow participants to consider the various degrees of danger associated with both medical and illegal drugs, allied to the way in which they are used, the reasons for use, and the environment in which they are used.

Purpose and expected outcomes

- To increase awareness of the potential danger involved in certain behaviour.
- To increase the participants' understanding of the possible outcomes of such behaviour.
- To encourage individual responsibility over drug decisions.
- To challenge attitudes to drug use.
- To reinforce drug prevention messages.

Method

The 'safety', 'danger', and 'midway' positioning cards should first be laid out on a floor or other flat surface, allowing sufficient space in between for all of the situation cards. The situation cards should be handed out individually to the participants, who are working either on their own or in pairs. Alternatively, they can be asked to choose one card at random. They should then be asked to consider the possible problems and dangers of the action written on the card, and to place their card in what they consider to be the right position between the safety and danger positioning cards. Those that are considered the most or least dangerous should be placed closest to the appropriate card. As they place their card, each participant is asked to justify their reasons for positioning the card where they have. Discussion within the whole group may follow and cards may be repositioned as necessary. If space is limited, the safety ladder sheet can be used as a handout, and students asked to write the number of the situation card in the appropriate position on the ladder. Alternatively the ladder sheet can be reproduced as an OHP slide and projected onto a white board. The numbers can then be written on the white board in the appropriate positions.

Notes for teacher or group leader

The accompanying notes refer to the numbered cards, and will assist the leader in discussing with the group the most appropriate position of each card.

Card 1

Possibility of overdose, danger from adulterants, danger from blood-borne infections (HIV, hepatitis etc.), may miss vein and hit artery or nerve, vein collapse, immediate and irreversible effect of the drug.

Card 2

More carcinogenic than tobacco alone, may cause drowsiness, hallucinations, lack of co-ordination, menstruation problems in female users, impotency problems in male users, may cause flashbacks if previous LSD user.

Card 3

Danger from asphyxiation, danger from heart failure, explosion if near naked flame, inhalation of vomit, collapse, accident, no help at hand, risk of sudden death.

Card 4

Totally safe!

Card 5

Many fake steroids on market, testicles may shrink permanently, in females clitoris may enlarge, use can cause aggression ('roid rages'), use associated with cancers, liver damage and personality changes.

Card 6

Friend may panic, have bad experience, become involved in an accident, be permanently affected, test positive for drugs.

Card 7

May collect wrong kind, nausea and vomiting, if prepared for use they become a class 'A' drug.

Card 8

Danger from overheating, dehydration, others around may be unaware, psychiatric problems, may cause death.

Card 9

Drowsiness, nausea, confusion, overheating.

Card 10

Depletes blood sugar, overconfidence, appetite suppressed, weight loss, immune system impairment, withdrawal symptoms include panic, anxiety and insomnia, tolerance may develop.

Card 11

Uncertain effects of mixing drugs, taking similar types of drug may cause overdose, cocktail may prove lethal, effect of one may cancel out that of another or cause new and unpredictable effect.

Card 12

Uncertain effects of mixing drugs, taking drugs with similar properties may cause overdose, cocktail may prove lethal effects of one may cancel out that of another or cause new and unpredictable effect.

Card 13

Unknown effect of new drug, may be 'snidey' pseudo drug.

Card 14

Sweet fruity taste masks alcohol content making it possible to drink too much and become drunk.

Card 15

Unknown content of capsules, may be dangerous substance, if friends adversely affected you could be held legally responsible.

Card 16

Seven per cent purity means 93% of impurities and other unknown substances. Injecting could lead to vein collapse, abscesses etc.

Card 17

Seventy per cent purity is much higher than normal street strength and could easily lead to overdose and death. Thirty per cent impurities can still cause problems, collapsed veins, abscesses etc.

Card 18

It is possible to overdose on tranquillisers and sleeping tablets, both types can easily become addictive, neither will remove the cause of the stress.

Card 19

Danger of asphyxiation, especially if bag is placed over the head or over nose and mouth.

Card 20

Alcohol and cannabis are both depressant drugs and their use together will exacerbate those depressant qualities, drowsiness, loss of co-ordination, slowing of bodily functions, risk of hallucinations. Parents could be charged with permitting the smoking of cannabis at home (maximum penalty: 14 years).

Card 21

Having a larger quantity of street drugs on you than would seem usual for a single individual could lead to a charge of possession with intent to supply, leading to a greater sentence.

Card 22

Crack cocaine is habit-forming, leading to increasing use and therefore costing larger sums of money at each usage due to developing tolerance. Full chemical addiction can develop in short time.

Card 23

Many impurities and adulterants, dangers of injecting, abscesses, dirty 'hits', collapsed veins etc. Class 'A' drug attracting heavy penalties, danger from overdose, risk of HIV/hepatitis B and C/gonorrhoea if needles or other injecting equipment (filters, spoons or even water) are shared. Danger of disposed needles to people and animals.

Card 24

More alcohol readily available, may get carried away in atmosphere.

Card 25

Use of drugs will not cure loneliness and may add to depression, cause other problems such as paranoia, insomnia, anxiety and debt, plus legal problems.

Card 26

Both drugs are powerful depressants and their use together can easily cause overdose and death.

Card 27

Too much paracetamol is toxic to the kidneys and liver, and overuse can cause permanent damage even leading to death in some cases. Tolerance may build up.

Card 28

Unknown effects on new user, effects may vary with mood of user and their environment etc. Trip could be good or horrendous, danger of life long flashbacks, danger of short- or long-term psychiatric problems. Class 'A' drug.

Card 29

Throat tissues may swell causing asphyxiation, fumes may ignite if someone smoking nearby.

Card 30

Uncertain effects of mixing drugs, one drug may cancel effect of the other, withdrawal symptoms to both drugs may combine, overdose possible if more drugs are taken.

Follow-up exercises

1. Collecting media articles on drug incidents where danger has been caused.
2. Essay covering differing aspects of drug use and the associated dangers.
3. Further group discussion of issues raised during exercise.

1.

INJECTING DRUGS USING A SHARED NEEDLE AND SYRINGE

2.

SMOKING CANNABIS IN A HAND-ROLLED CIGARETTE

3.

SNIFFING LIGHTER FUEL ALONE IN AN ISOLATED PLACE

4.

NOT USING ANY ILLEGAL DRUG OR INTOXICATING SUBSTANCE

5.

INJECTING ANABOLIC STEROIDS TO HELP BUILD MUSCLE BULK

6.

PUTTING AN LSD TRIP IN A FRIEND'S DRINK WITHOUT THEM KNOWING

7.

COLLECTING, PREPARING AND USING MAGIC MUSHROOMS

8.

USING BOTH ECSTASY AND SPEED IN A CROWDED DANCE CLUB

9.

SNIFFING 'POPPERS' HANDED TO YOU AT A PARTY

10.

TAKING SPEED TO GIVE YOU ENERGY

11.

TAKING VARIOUS DRUGS AT THE SAME TIME

12.

USING STREET DRUGS WHILST TAKING MEDICATION PRESCRIBED BY YOUR DOCTOR

13.

USING A 'HOWLING WOLF' OR A 'GRIZZLY BEAR', NEW DRUGS ON THE SCENE, RECOMMENDED BY A DEALER

14.

DRINKING ALCO-POPS AT HOME

15.

SELLING PINK CAPSULES THAT YOU FOUND IN THE STREET TO YOUR FRIENDS

16.

INJECTING A POWDER DRUG THAT IS ONLY 7% PURE

17.

INJECTING A POWDER DRUG THAT IS 70% PURE

18.

USING TRANQUILLISERS AND SLEEPING TABLETS BECAUSE YOU ARE STRESSED

19.

SNIFFING A VOLATILE SUBSTANCE FROM A PLASTIC BAG

20.

USING ALCOHOL AND CANNABIS IN YOUR BEDROOM AT YOUR PARENTS' HOUSE

21.

BUYING STREET DRUGS ON BEHALF OF FRIENDS WHO GAVE YOU THE MONEY

22.

SMOKING CRACK COCAINE CRYSTALS

23.

INJECTING STREET HEROIN

24.

DRINKING ALCOHOL IN A PUB

25.

TAKING STREET DRUGS BECAUSE YOU FEEL DEPRESSED AND LONELY

26.

USING HEROIN AND ALCOHOL AT THE SAME TIME

27.

TAKING MORE PARACETAMOL THAN IS ADVISED ON THE BOTTLE

28.

TRYING LSD FOR THE FIRST TIME TO SEE IF YOU LIKE IT

29.

SQUIRTING LIGHTER FUEL DIRECTLY INTO THE MOUTH AND THROAT

30.

USING BOTH A STIMULANT AND A DEPRESSANT DRUG AT THE SAME TIME (e.g. SPEED AND HEROIN)

DANGER

SAFE

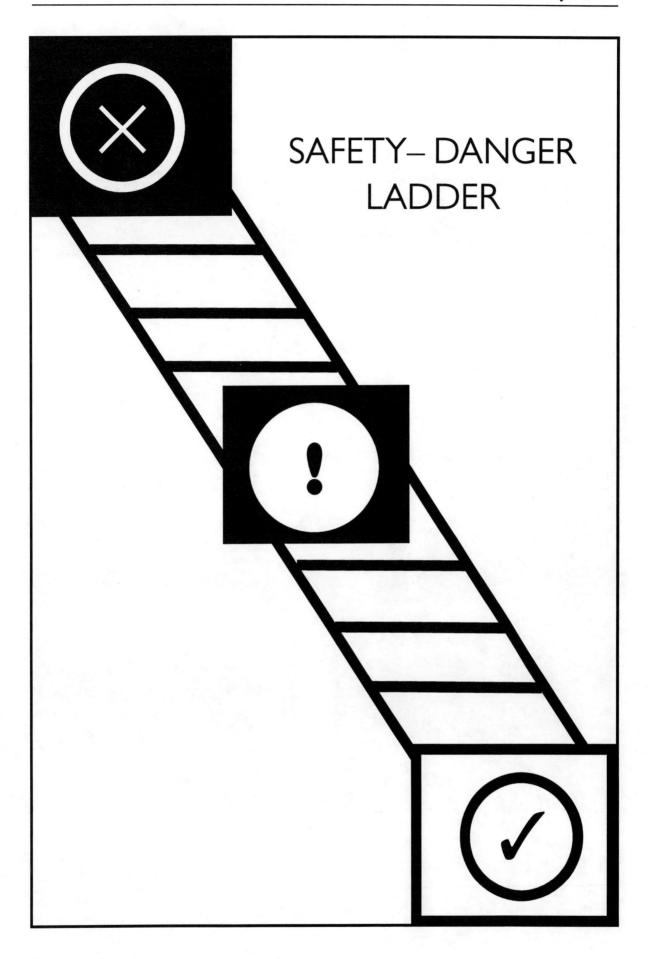

SAFETY– DANGER
LADDER

Slang

Suggested age: 14+

Outline

An exercise that allows participants to improve their knowledge and understanding of drugs and their use, by exploring the subject of drug-related slang.

Purpose and expected outcome

- To improve knowledge and understanding of drugs and their use.
- To demystify drug slang by increasing understanding.
- To deglamourise drug slang by exploring its meaning and origins.
- To challenge attitudes to drug use.
- To reinforce drug prevention messages.

Method

The worksheets contain 30 slang words or phrases that are associated with drugs and their use. The sheets can be copied, cut up and laminated for use, or simply used as sources for the teacher or leader to read out to participants. The participants should be divided into groups of four or five, and issued with a number of the slang cards for consideration. If the sheet is being used as a source, then a number of pieces of slang can be read to each group for the members to write down. Each group's consideration should include what the members understand the word or phrase to mean, and whether there is more than one meaning. The group should also consider where it believes the piece of slang originated and how it got its present meaning. Following sufficient time for discussion, the groups should report their results to the rest of the class. The leader can write the slang words on the board, together with the meaning and origins that the group has agreed upon. General discussion, issues raised, and further thoughts from the rest of the class should be encouraged and included on the board. When all of the groups have reported back, the leader should draw together the various issues that have been raised and explore with the class whether the pieces of slang present positive or negative images. The exercise also includes a word search game containing 15 pieces of drug slang. This can be used as a short introduction to the subject of slang or as a follow on activity.

Notes for teacher or group leader

Generally accepted meanings and origins of the slang words and phrases.

DOPE

Meaning – Cannabis, occasionally drugs in general.
Origins – From its literal meaning, viz: 'anything supplied to dull, blind or blunt the conscience or insight'; also from its colloquial meaning of a person who is of low intellect, a dullard or a fool.

CRASH

Meaning – To come down from the effects of a stimulant drug.
Origins – From its literal meaning, viz: 'to fall or rush to destruction and collapse, to fail or fall apart'.

COLD TURKEY

Meaning – The process of withdrawing from heroin without medical help, occasionally applied to withdrawal from other drugs.
Origins – During withdrawal from heroin without assistance from prescribed medications, the skin of the withdrawer goes through a series of rapid fluctuations in temperature. When the skin is cold it has a clammy feel and is covered in goose pimples. This can give it the appearance of the plucked skin of a dead turkey.

BUSTED

Meaning – Being searched and/or arrested by the police for drug offences. Also applied to having your house, room or car searched by the police.
Origins – From its literal meaning, viz: 'broken, no longer in working order, bankrupt'.

UPPERS

Meaning – Any stimulant drug, particularly one in tablet form.

Origins – From the ability of stimulants to lift the user both psychologically and physically.

HOOKED

Meaning – To be addicted, either physically or psychologically, to a drug.
Origins – From its literal meaning, viz: 'ensnared upon a hook'. An efficient hook is fitted with a barb to prevent the object that it has ensnared becoming easily unhooked.

SKUNK

Meaning – A form of cannabis produced by cross-breeding different strains of the cannabis plant to produce high levels of the active ingredient, delta 9 tetrahydrocannabinol. This variety was first produced in Holland and is also called 'Nederweed'.
Origins – From the unpleasant smell that is produced when it is smoked, said to resemble the pungent spray used by the skunk as a form of defence.

CRACK BABY

Meaning – The baby born to a mother who has used crack cocaine throughout pregnancy. The baby will be born withdrawing from the drug and in a distressed state, and also is at risk of being born physically or intellectually damaged.
Origin – The word 'crack' is applied to the crystalline form of cocaine because of the noise that the crystals make when they are heated for smoking.

HIGH

Meaning – The effects felt by a person using a stimulant drug such as amphetamine or cocaine. Sometimes applied to the effects of non-stimulant drugs.
Origin – From the ability of stimulants to lift the user both psychologically and physically.

FLASHBACK

Meaning – The re-run of a hallucinogenic experience or 'trip' without further use of a drug. Flashbacks are a common feature of LSD use, but can also occur with other hallucinogens such as 'magic mushrooms'. They can occur weeks, months or even years after use of the drug has finished.
Origin – From the cinematic technique of showing scenes from a person's past during the course of the narrative.

LOVE DOVE

Meaning – An ecstasy tablet with a dove motif imprinted into its surface.

Origins – Ecstasy can increase the user's empathy towards others and also their libido. These two effects can lead to a physical and emotional attraction or feelings of love towards others.

LOSING THE PLOT

Meaning – Becoming totally confused or losing all ambition or interest in life, usually as a result of cannabis use. Sometimes applied to a similar effect from the use or withdrawal from other drugs.

Origin – From the meaning of the word 'plot' viz: 'the story or scheme of connected events running through a play, novel, etc'.

DOWNERS

Meaning – Any depressant drug, commonly applied to tablet forms of such drugs as tranquillisers.

Origins – From the ability of depressant drugs to lower or slow down the user both emotionally and physically.

RUSH

Meaning – The onset of effects from drug use, usually stimulants, also applied to the rapid effect from injecting drugs.

Origins – From its literal meaning, viz: 'to move forward with haste, impetuosity or rashness' or 'to force out of place; to hasten or hustle forward'.

SNIDEY

Meaning – Something that is sold under the pretence that it is a particular drug, but is actually something else. Is often applied to tablets sold falsely as ecstasy.

Origins – From the literal meaning of the word 'snide', viz: 'sham; counterfeit; base; mean; dishonest; derogatory in an insinuating way; showing malice'.

TRACK MARKS

Meanings – The scars left on the skin surface by injecting drugs.

Origins – From the literal meaning of the word 'track', viz: 'a mark or trail left or a sequence or course of actions'.

ROID RAGE

Meaning – A sudden fit of uncontrollable aggression as a side effect of using anabolic steroids. These outbursts of aggression can often have sexual overtones and lead to the user committing violent sexual crimes.

Origin – An example of alliteration applied to drug slang, 'roid' is a shortened version of steroid.

SPEED FREAK

Meaning – A habituated user of amphetamine.
Origins – 'Speed' is the drug slang for amphetamine. The second part of the phrase comes from the literal meaning of the word 'freak', viz: 'a monstrosity; an eccentric; a weirdly unconventional person; a person who is wildly enthusiastic about something'.

TAB

Meaning – A small square of paper impregnated with the drug LSD, and with a pictogram printed upon it. May also be short for tablet.
Origins – From its literal meaning, viz: 'a small label'.

TRIPS

Meaning – Small squares of paper impregnated with the hallucinogenic drug LSD, and with pictograms printed upon them
Origins – From its literal meaning, viz: 'to make a journey', describing the hallucinatory experience.

HASH

Meaning – Short for hashish, a name for cannabis resin.
Origins – From the Arabic word 'hasheesh', which in turn is derived from an Indian dialect word 'haschishin', the name for a nineteenth-century group of assassins who made use of the drug.

ECSTASY

Meaning – A name for MDMA, a hallucinogenic stimulant drug.
Origins – From its literal meaning, viz: 'a state of exalted pleasure or happiness or rapture', describing the effects that the user is seeking.

WACKY BACCY

Meaning – A name applied to herbal cannabis.
Origins – From the literal meaning of 'wacky', viz: 'crazy or zany', together with 'baccy', short for tobacco.

RESIN

Meaning – Applied to a solid form of cannabis
Origins – From its literal meaning, viz: 'a substance derived from the sap of a plant'.

JUNKIE

Meaning – A drug user, more specifically a person who is addicted to drugs, especially heroin, which is sometimes known as junk.

Origins – Derived from the use of the word in the USA as slang for 'a lunatic', also from the word 'junk' meaning 'worthless rubbish'.

MUSHIES

Meaning – Hallucinogenic or 'magic' mushrooms.

Origins – Simply an altered form of the word 'mushroom'.

COMEDOWN

Meaning – The feelings of withdrawing from a drug, or simply the feelings experienced as the effects subside.

Origins – From its literal meaning, viz: 'a descent; a disappointment or deflation; a degradation'.

SPIKE

Meaning – A hypodermic needle, sometimes applied to both the syringe and needle; or to contaminate food or drink by the addition of a harmful substance.

Origins – From its literal meaning, viz: 'a hard pointed object' and to pierce, damage or make useless.

PUSHER

Meaning – A dealer in or supplier of drugs.

Origins – From the actions of suppliers of drugs 'pushing' them onto their customers. Today, the pressure usually comes from the customer, the supplier having little need to push as the demand is so great. The real pusher is often a young person who encourages friends to experiment with drugs.

SPEED

Meaning – Amphetamine sulphate.

Origins – From the stimulation that the user experiences, causing a speeding up of the body's metabolism; also from its literal meaning, viz: to drive at high, or at dangerously, unduly, or illegally high, speed.

Follow-up exercises

Collecting other examples of slang words that apply to things other than drugs. The word-search sheet can also be used.

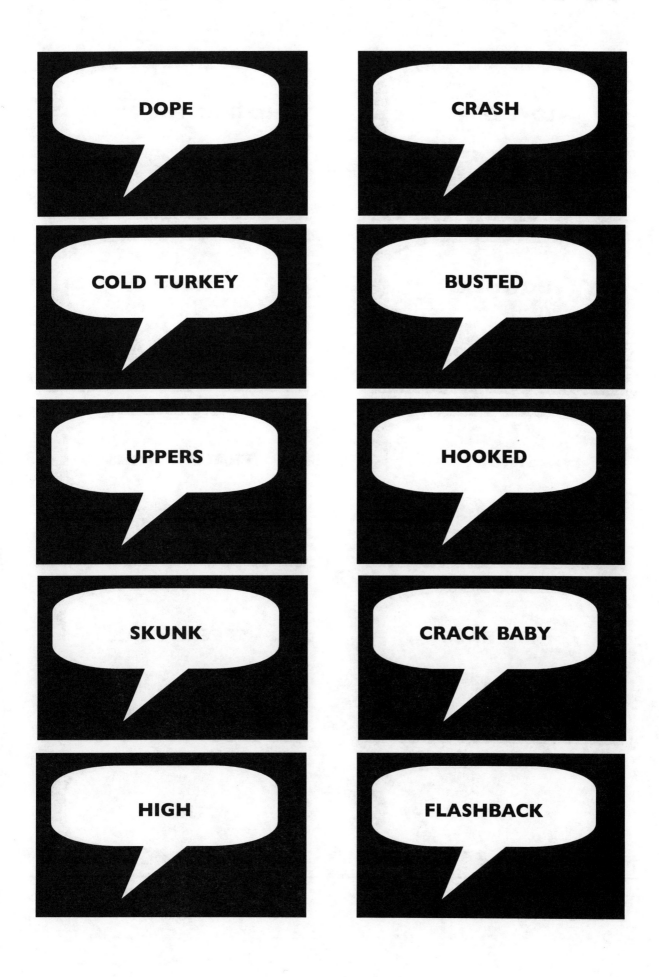

LOVE DOVE

LOSING THE PLOT

DOWNERS

RUSH

SNIDEY

TRACK MARKS

ROID RAGE

SPEED FREAK

TAB

TRIPS

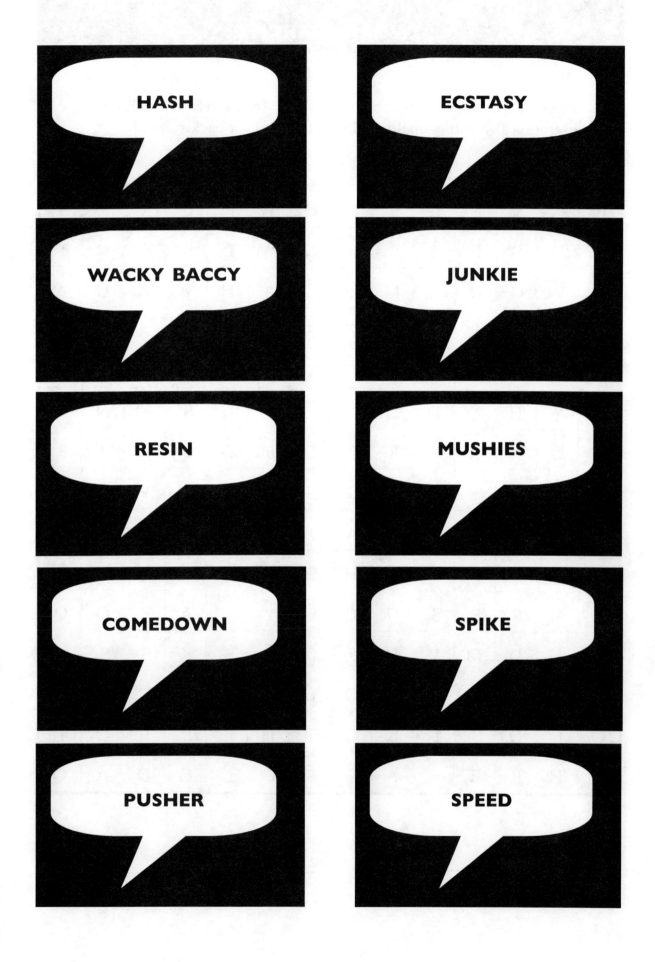

WORD SEARCH

The grid contains 15 examples of drug slang. They can be found horizontally, vertically or diagonally and read forwards or backwards.

F	G	M	E	L	S	D	O	W	N	E	R	S	S
J	D	D	F	A	U	P	O	W	L	S	S	C	T
N	W	O	D	E	M	O	C	A	H	W	A	H	A
G	U	P	T	R	I	P	S	C	L	F	A	E	B
A	O	E	T	E	I	J	S	K	N	U	K	S	R
Y	Y	H	C	H	O	I	I	Y	L	S	M	N	N
E	U	N	G	S	R	I	D	B	D	S	A	I	F
K	E	E	Y	U	T	I	E	A	D	M	V	D	E
R	U	G	I	P	O	A	T	C	X	Z	I	E	L
U	S	A	J	P	Y	H	S	C	R	W	Q	Y	D
T	K	R	E	S	C	C	U	Y	I	A	P	O	O
D	U	D	M	V	D	E	B	F	S	K	S	S	W
L	T	I	W	J	I	D	L	V	R	B	T	H	L
O	L	O	S	I	N	G	T	H	E	P	L	O	T
C	H	R	R	B	A	E	K	O	N	G	D	A	Q

WORD SEARCH ANSWER SHEET

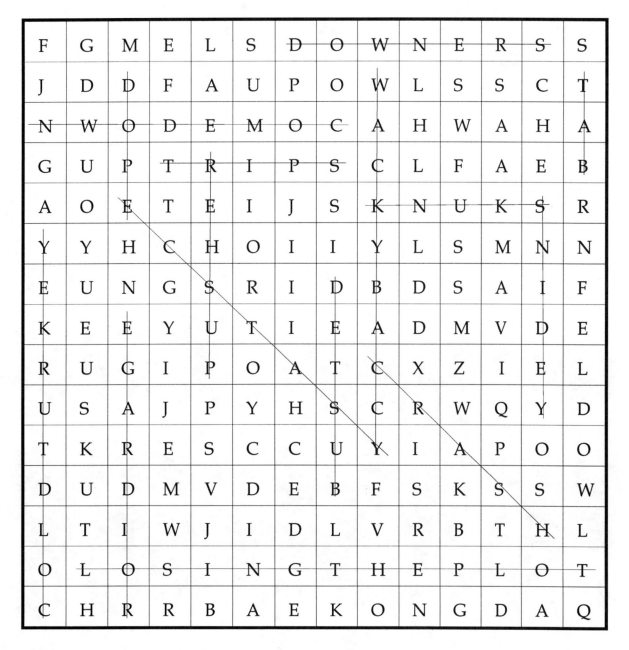

F	G	M	E	L	S	D	O	W	N	E	R	S	S
J	D	D	F	A	U	P	O	W	L	S	S	C	T
N	W	O	D	E	M	O	C	A	H	W	A	H	A
G	U	P	T	R	I	P	S	C	L	F	A	E	B
A	O	E	T	E	I	J	S	K	N	U	K	S	R
Y	Y	H	C	H	O	I	I	Y	L	S	M	N	N
E	U	N	G	S	R	I	D	B	D	S	A	I	F
K	E	E	Y	U	T	I	E	A	D	M	V	D	E
R	U	G	I	P	O	A	T	C	X	Z	I	E	L
U	S	A	J	P	Y	H	S	C	R	W	Q	Y	D
T	K	R	E	S	C	C	U	Y	I	A	P	O	O
D	U	D	M	V	D	E	B	F	S	K	S	S	W
L	T	I	W	J	I	D	L	V	R	B	T	H	L
O	L	O	S	I	N	G	T	H	E	P	L	O	T
C	H	R	R	B	A	E	K	O	N	G	D	A	Q

DOPE	TRIPS	DOWNERS	TAB
WACKY BACCY	COMEDOWN	SKUNK	COLD TURKEY
PUSHER	BUSTED	SNIDEY	CRASH
LOSING THE PLOT	ECSTASY	ROID RAGE	

Check It Out

Suggested age: 14+

Outline

A quiz in 'true or false' format, designed to allow participants to check out their knowledge of drugs and drug use. Suggested length of exercise: one hour.

Purpose and expected outcome

- To provide accurate information about drugs and drug use.
- To balance the very largely pro-drug slant of most 'street' information.
- To encourage individual responsibility over drug decisions.
- To challenge attitudes to drug use.
- To reinforce drug prevention messages.

Method

The quiz sheets contain 35 questions designed to be suitable for young people aged 14 years and above. They all require answers of the true or false type. They have been produced as two pages of ten questions each and a further sheet of 15 questions. The teacher or leader can decide on the length of the quiz to suit the time available.

It should be explained to the participants that the purpose of the quiz is not to examine their level of knowledge about drugs and drug use, but rather to enable them to check out the accuracy of the knowledge that they already have, and to add useful and balanced information.

The quiz sheets should be copied and handed out to the participants, and time allowed for them to answer the questions. The teacher or leader should then go through the answers using the following guidance notes. Many of the questions will prompt discussion of associated drug issues. This is intended, and should be encouraged.

Participants should be asked to correct their sheets in line with the given answers and keep them for future reference.

Notes for teacher or group leader

SUGGESTED ANSWERS:

1. (a) **True** – Put simply, the bigger you are then the more of a particular drug you will need for a particular effect. A person with a large body mass will have a greater quantity of blood to dilute the drug and also a greater number of cells to spread the drug across. One exception to this is LSD: with this drug, the most powerful hallucinogenic substance known, there does not seem to be a close link between required dosage and body mass. Different people do react differently to the same size dose of LSD, but this is the result of other more complicated factors to do with mood and brain chemistry, rather than simple body weight.

    (b) **True** – The average woman is smaller than the average man. There are also many hormonal differences that mean that women deal with some drugs differently. Hormonal differences, for example, mean that women process many drugs more slowly and so retain them within the body longer than men.

    (c) **True** – The mood of the user when taking the drug will often have a direct effect on the outcome. This effect is particularly noticeable with hallucinogenic drugs, such as LSD or magic mushrooms, but will also be seen in the use of mind or mood altering drugs, such as cannabis, alcohol, ecstasy. Drug users will often refer to their mood on using a drug as their 'mind set'. Users who take their drugs in circumstances and company that are safe and secure, and in which they feel relaxed and happy, will have a good 'mind set' and be more likely to have a pleasant experience than if the circumstances and company are stressful or insecure and the user feels under stress, threatened or unhappy. In these circumstances the outcome is more likely to be unpleasant or frightening.

    (d) **True** – The method used to administer the drug will directly influence the effects that are achieved. Injecting the drug into a vein will result in the most profound effects, as this method introduces the drug directly and immediately into the bloodstream, and from there it will reach the brain within a matter of two or three seconds at the most. Smoking a drug is the second quickest method of introducing it into your blood system, providing the method of smoking does not cause the drug to be weakened or even destroyed. Taking a drug by mouth is the slowest method of introducing it into the body and generally will achieve the least profound effects.

(e) **True** – Previous use of any drug will mean that tolerance will have begun to develop, this is particularly true with regular use; tolerance meaning that the user requires more and more of the drug to achieve a certain level of effects as regular use continues.

2. **False** – Addiction or dependence, either physical or psychological, can develop to any drug through regular use by any method.

3. **True** – The effects of withdrawal from heroin use without medical help can be described as being like a bout of the worst 'flu that you can imagine. This, of course, only describes the physical symptoms, the psychological cravings for the drug can be extremely powerful. It needs emphasising that the vast majority of addicted heroin users do not recover to become drug-free. Addicted users have a less than one in ten chance of a complete recovery.

4. **True** – Tolerance develops to all drugs with regular use; tolerance meaning that the user requires more and more of the drug to achieve a certain level of effect, as regular use continues.

5. **True** – These can be both physical and psychological. Their intensity will be dependent upon the amount and regularity of alcohol use. These symptoms can range from trembling limbs, lack of concentration and headaches to unbearable cravings and hallucinations (delirium tremens).

6. **False** – Intense intoxication from alcohol takes a relatively long time to develop, and a much longer time to pass. A dose of alcohol takes around one hour to be fully absorbed by the body and is cleared from the system at the rate of approximately one unit (10ml absolute alcohol) per hour. Intense intoxication from solvent abuse can come on within a matter of seconds of commencing the use of the solvent. With powerful solvents such as liquid petroleum gas, intense intoxication will be felt within 20 to 30 seconds. The chemicals are readily absorbed by the user's bloodstream but are also rapidly given up. An intoxicated solvent user will return to sobriety within a short time, around 30 minutes on average. This difference in the time taken to go from sober to intoxicated and back again between alcohol and solvents only serves to emphasise the very real differences between the two methods of achieving intoxication.

7. **True** – When most of the substances being sniffed were solvent glues and liquid solvents, the majority of deaths were caused by accidents that the user became involved in due to their intoxicated state. With the increase in the misuse of liquid petroleum gas (LPG) and aerosols propelled by LPG, this has changed. The majority of deaths are now due directly to the effects of such products. LPG causes sudden death in two common ways: the extreme cold

produced by releasing the pressurised gas directly into the throat causes the throat and larynx tissues to swell causing asphyxiation; and LPG also causes the overproduction of the hormone adrenaline which can lead to over stimulation of the heart and heart failure.

8. **False** – A commonly held belief that is now very much out of date. Use of cannabis can lead directly to cancers of the mouth, tongue, throat and lungs. Its use can be a causational factor in certain mental illnesses, including schizophrenia and psychosis. In females it can cause disruption of the menstrual cycle and damage to an unborn foetus. In males it can lead to reduction in testosterone levels and associated impotency problems. Cannabis is as yet little understood and new problems are emerging as investigation about it continues.

9. **True** – In the sense that it can damage the normal operation of the brain. Use of LSD can produce powerful hallucinations for the user that can cause deep psychological trauma. Its use can activate latent mental illnesses that might have remained inactive without its use. Many users also experience 'flashbacks' weeks, months or even years after using LSD. A 'flashback' is a rerun of the trip without further use of the drug. These reruns are usually of shorter duration but can be very distressing. They can occur at any time and often without warning, placing the sufferer, and perhaps those around them, in serious danger.

10. **False** – Ecstasy or MDMA has been the direct cause of a large number of deaths involving young people. The drug can cause sudden death in a number of ways, overheating leading to convulsions and collapse and strokes caused by the formation of blood clots being perhaps the most common. Any user also needs to take into account the potential that the use of ecstasy has for activating latent mental illnesses and causing profound changes in personality. Tolerance to the drug quickly builds up leading to the need for higher and higher doses which increases the chance of an adverse reaction. The drug is noted for its unpredictability and previous safe use of it does not mean that any future use will be similarly safe.

11. **True** – Many users experience 'flashbacks' weeks, months or even years after using LSD. A 'flashback' is a rerun of the hallucinogenic trip without further use of the drug. These reruns are usually of shorter duration but can be very distressing. They can occur at any time and often without warning, placing the sufferer, and perhaps those around them, in serious danger. Research indicates that a person who uses cannabis in the same time period during which they use LSD will have an increased risk of suffering flashbacks.

12. **False** – The act of injecting drugs alone will not infect any one with HIV. Sharing injecting equipment with any one who is infected

with HIV will place the user at great risk of becoming similarly infected. Injecting equipment includes not only the needle and syringe but also the spoon or other vessel used to prepare the drug for injection. All such equipment can easily become contaminated with infected blood. Free issues of clean needles and syringes are available in almost all areas in order to reduce the risk of this type of infection.

13. **True** – Experiments were carried out in the 1920s and early 1930s in the UK, and in the 1960s in the USA, to test the possibility of using ecstasy (MDMA) as a treatment for certain psychiatric illnesses. The drug proved of little benefit and extremely unpredictable in its side effects, and has no permitted medical use.

14. **True** – Ecstasy is a class A drug, and supply of the same carries a maximum penalty on indictment of life imprisonment together with an unlimited fine and the confiscation of any drug related assets.

15. **True** – Cannabis is a class B drug and possession carries a maximum penalty on indictment of five years' imprisonment and an unlimited fine.

16. **True** – Amphetamine (speed) use carries a very real risk of serious and often permanent damage to psychiatric health. Many users become depressed and anxious after using for only a short time. Longer use can lead to paranoia, delusions and psychosis. Often these illnesses will require inpatient treatment in psychiatric hospitals and can prove difficult if not impossible to cure.

17. **False** – Cannabis contains some 50 per cent more recognised cancer-causing substances than tobacco. Its smoke is much hotter and more tar-laden than tobacco, and has a potential for causing cancer that is at least as high if not higher than tobacco.

18. **False** – If figures are examined for the population as a whole, the percentage of people who have ever used an illegal drug drops down into single figures. It is only in today's youth generation that the figures become significantly high. The scale of the current use of drugs by young people is a totally new phenomenon. No generation within recorded history has used drugs on this scale before: it is impossible to predict what the outcome is likely to be.

19. **False** – The offence of supplying requires only that an illegal drug is supplied to another person, it does not require the exchange of any money or other form of payment. A person giving a drug to someone as a gift commits the offence of supplying. Even sharing a cannabis cigarette with someone counts as supplying. Supplying drugs carries the highest penalties of all drug offences.

20. **False** – Possession of fresh and unprocessed magic mushrooms is not an offence under the drug legislation. Any act of preparing them for consumption, such as drying, cooking or chopping, means that they

become controlled substances under class A of the Misuse of Drugs Act (1931) and attract the same penalties as heroin. Picking wild magic mushrooms for your own use or for sale, on land that belongs to someone else, without the landowner's permission, can be an offence under the Theft Act (1968).

21. **False** – A person would need a good level of knowledge of fungi to positively identify members of the magic mushroom group when seen growing. When they have been dried it would require the services of a laboratory to correctly identify them. Many of the problems caused by magic mushrooms are caused by a person using the wrong varieties, many of which are highly toxic.

22. **True and False** – This depends upon your gender. In females the clitoris can become very enlarged and painfully sensitive, in males steroid use can cause the genitalia to shrink. These changes can become permanent.

23. **False** – Cannabis use can lead to a powerful psychological dependency. The authors of this quiz have dealt with cannabis users who could not get out of bed in the morning without smoking the drug first; they felt unable to face the world without its use. This use of the drug then continued throughout the day.

24. **False** – Ecstasy is a class A drug like heroin.

25. **False** – Most drugs sold on the streets have been mixed or 'cut' with other substances in order to increase their weight and bulk and therefore the dealers' profit levels. Some of these 'cutting' agents can be harmless, such as milk powder, glucose, vitamin C powder and so on, whilst others can be very dangerous. Substances such as chalk, talcum powder, brick dust, cleaning agents, fertilizers, rodent poisons or other drugs have frequently been found. The purity levels of street drugs can vary considerably, making their effects difficult to predict. Many users have suffered fatal overdoses as a result of buying a drug at an unusually high level of purity.

26. **False** – It would be very dangerous to rely on this. It is true to say that most police forces caution persons arrested in possession of small amounts of drugs for their own personal use, but this is not guaranteed. There will be circumstances in which they will consider a court appearance to be more appropriate. Cautions are increasingly used for the first such offence only, and any subsequent arrests will almost certainly lead to a court appearance. If found guilty in court, the user will have acquired a drugs criminal record; such a record may prove an insurmountable obstacle to many choices of career. The armed services, the civil service, most local government and many companies will not employ people with such a record. Many foreign countries will not issue work or residential permits to convicted drug users and some will not even issue a visa to visit on holiday.

27. **True** – The act of injecting brings with it many problems. Using injecting equipment that has been used by other people lays the user open to contracting any infection that the previous user has. Infections such as HIV, hepatitis B and C, septicemia and gonorrhoea, are commonly passed in this way. Injecting impure drugs that contain solids can cause blocked veins, leading to vein collapse and gangrene. Injection sites frequently become infected and abscesses are common. The injected drug enters directly into the blood system and reaches the central nervous system within seconds. Once injected it cannot be removed and any overdosing is difficult to counter. With drugs taken orally the excess can often be pumped or washed from the stomach.

28. **False** – The withdrawal effects of amphetamine use will vary according to the amount that the user has been taking and the duration and regularity of the use. Most inexperienced users who have only taken a small to moderate amount of amphetamine will experience a period of tiredness and loss of strength. This can be dealt with by allowing the body to rest, sleep being the best way of doing so. If the use of the drug has been at a much higher level or over an extended period the withdrawal effects will be much more severe. Many such users will find it extremely difficult to cope with the feelings of anxiety, panic, paranoia and insomnia that such withdrawal will bring. Anyone attempting to give up the use of amphetamine after heavy or prolonged use is well advised to seek the advice and guidance of a professional drug service.

29. **True** – It is impossible to overstate the power of heroin. It is very difficult, if not impossible, for most users to prevent themselves becoming addicted, both chemically and psychologically, to the drug. In the UK over 90 per cent of addicted heroin users never succeed in becoming drug-free. People tempted to try heroin need to be very clear about this: the 'power of the powder' is likely to be much stronger than they are, and once they begin heroin use they are entering a world that can be impossible to escape.

30. **True** – Any drug used by a pregnant woman will also enter the bloodstream of the unborn infant. Crack cocaine causes especially severe problems if used by pregnant women. Many of these will suffer spontaneous abortions due to placental displacement. Many babies will be stillborn. The chief cause of these problems is the way in which all forms of cocaine restrict the flow of blood along veins and arteries, which significantly reduces the volume of blood flowing through the umbilical cord into the foetus. This reduction together with the consequent reduction in oxygen supply often leads to the baby being born either physically or neurological damaged, or both. Some of this damage can be extreme. No figures for such births are available for the UK but it has been estimated that some two per cent of births in the USA are to crack-using

mothers. Even if the child is lucky enough to avoid any pre-birth damage, it is likely to be born withdrawing from crack use, which will be extremely unpleasant and potentially very dangerous for it.

31. **True** – The withdrawal effects of many drugs can lead to aggression on the part of the user. This is true of most stimulants, and especially true of crack cocaine. The feelings can be very unpleasant and can easily lead to uncontrollable outbursts of aggression. Such outbursts are a regular feature of the use of anabolic steroids. So common are they that they are given a special name, 'roid rages', these can be very spectacular and include a sexual element in the aggression which can lead the user to commit violent sexual crimes.

32. **True** – Using two drugs of a similar nature, such as two stimulants or depressants, can lead to overdose. Mixing drugs of differing natures can lead to unpredictable and often dangerous results.

33. **False** – The dilation of the blood vessels within the body caused by the inhalation of 'poppers' leads to a dramatic reduction in blood pressure. The heart beat rises in an attempt to maintain adequate blood pressure. Severe dizziness and blackouts together with nausea and vomiting are common. These factors together increase the risk of the user inhaling his/her own vomit and choking to death. There have been reports of strokes and heart attacks following extensive use of poppers among people who may have had some underlying defect in their cardiovascular system. Some users report that their use of poppers leaves them with severe headaches and sore eyes. Poppers can cause a variety of skin problems including dermatitis, they can also cause damage to the eyes if it comes into contact with them and the drinking of the product can lead to severe poisoning.

34. **False** – At the time of writing there are no approved medical uses for cannabis. A number of areas of research are currently under way. Cannabis is being investigated as a possible drug for the alleviation of the nauseous effects of chemotherapy, as an appetite stimulant in wasting diseases, to reduce muscle spasm in multiple sclerosis and to reduce eyeball pressure in glaucoma sufferers. All of this research is ongoing and has not yet been concluded. Until it is, it would be unsafe to suggest that cannabis should be used medically in such cases. Medical history is littered with examples of drugs that appeared to have a beneficial part to play in combating certain conditions only to cause dangerous problems with unforeseen side-effects. Should cannabis show a beneficial effect in the treatment of these disorders it will be made available in a medical form, not in a smoking form. Even if it passes all the drug safety tests this would not mean that it is safe for others to use. Heroin has a respected place in the medical treatment of certain conditions; this does not mean that heroin is safe for others to use.

35. **True** – Between a quarter and a third of all the recorded solvent deaths each year in the UK are of people who have no previous history of solvent use. Solvents have a real potential to cause sudden death the first time that they are used.

Follow-up exercises

The quiz will have raised many issues connected with drug use. Any of these can be followed up with discussions, research projects or essay writing, or in any other way that the group leader sees as being appropriate and useful.

TRUE   FALSE

1. Effects of drugs are influenced by:
   (a) body weight;
   (b) gender;
   (c) mood;
   (d) method of use;
   (e) previous use.

2. Addiction only develops when drugs are injected.

3. Withdrawal from heroin is similar to a bout of 'flu.

4. Tolerance can develop to all drugs, including nicotine and alcohol.

5. There are withdrawal symptoms from alcohol.

6. Intoxication from sniffing solvents usually lasts for hours.

7. Most sniffing deaths are caused by the poisonous effects of the substance used.

8. There is no evidence of long-term harm from cannabis use.

9. LSD use can cause brain damage.

10. Ecstasy is a safe drug for recreational use.

TRUE   FALSE

11. Flashbacks are possible after LSD use.

12. Injecting drugs will give you HIV and Aids.

13. Ecstasy has been use medically in psychiatric hospitals.

14. The maximum penalty for giving one ecstasy tablet to a friend could be life imprisonment.

15. The maximum penalty for the possession of just one cannabis cigarette could be five years' imprisonment.

16. Amphetamine can cause personality disorders and mental illness.

17. Cannabis does not cause cancer.

18. Most people experiment with drugs at some time in their lives.

19. You have to sell drugs to others before you can be charged with supplying.

20. Magic mushrooms are not illegal.

21. It is easy to tell magic mushrooms from other more poisonous varieties.

22. Steroid use can enlarge your genitals.

TRUE FALSE

23. Cannabis is not addictive.

24. Ecstasy is a class B drug like cannabis.

25. Street drugs are generally pure.

26. The police only caution for possession of drugs these days.

27. Injecting is the most dangerous way to use any drug.

28. There are no withdrawal effects from amphetamine use.

29 If you get addicted to heroin you probably won't get off it.

30. Pregnant women who use crack are risking their babies' health.

31. Some drug use can cause aggression.

32. Mixing drugs is especially dangerous.

33. There are no ill-effects from using poppers.

34. Cannabis is used medically.

35. People have died the first time they sniffed solvents.

EXERCISE 6

Fact or Fiction?

Suggested age: 11+

Outline

A quiz in 'true or false' format, designed to allow participants to check out their knowledge of drugs and drug use. Suggested length of exercise: one hour.

Purpose and expected outcome

- To provide accurate information about drugs and drug use.
- To balance the very largely pro-drug slant of most 'street' information.
- To encourage individual responsibility over drug decisions.
- To challenge attitudes to drug use.
- To reinforce drug prevention messages.

Method

The quiz sheets contain 20 questions designed to be suitable for young people aged 11 years and above. They all require answers of the true or false type. They have been produced as two pages of ten questions each. The teacher or leader can decide on the length of the quiz to suit the time available.

It should be explained to the participants that the purpose of the quiz is not to examine their level of knowledge about drugs and drug use, but rather to enable them to check out the accuracy or otherwise of the knowledge that they already have and to add useful and balanced information.

The quiz sheets should be copied and handed out to the participants, and time allowed for them to answer the questions. The teacher or leader should then go through the answers using the following guidance notes. Many of the questions will prompt discussion of associated drug issues. This is intended and should be encouraged.

Participants should be asked to correct their sheets in line with the given answers and to keep them for future reference.

Notes for Teacher or Group Leader

SUGGESTED ANSWERS:

1. **False** – Dope, marijuana, grass and cannabis are all the same drug. All forms contain the same active ingredient, a complex substance called delta 9 tetrahydrocannabinol. There are some 200 names for cannabis in its various forms.

2. **True** – Ecstasy is not produced commercially anywhere in the world and consequently has no established form. It is produced illegally in a bewildering variety of shapes, sizes, forms and colours. It is very easy for users to be sold tablets and capsules as ecstasy that turn out to be other substances. These are known in drug slang as 'snideys', and may include very powerful and dangerous medical products.

3. **True** – Most drugs sold on the streets have been mixed or 'cut' with other substances in order to increase their weight and bulk, and therefore the dealers' profit levels. Some of these 'cutting' agents can be harmless, such as milk powder, glucose, vitamin C powder and so on, while others can be very dangerous. Substances such as chalk, talcum powder, brick dust, cleaning agents, fertilizers, rodent poisons or other drugs have frequently been used. The purity levels of street drugs can vary considerably, making their effects difficult to predict. Many users have suffered fatal overdoses as result of buying a drug at an unusually high level of purity.

4. **True** – Any user needs to take into account the potential that ecstasy use has for activating latent mental illnesses, such as psychosis and schizophrenia, and for causing profound changes in personality. Tolerance to the drug quickly builds up, leading to the need for higher and higher doses, which increases the chance of an adverse reaction. The drug is noted for its unpredictability, and previous safe use of it does not mean that any future use will be similarly safe. Ecstasy, or MDMA, has been the direct cause of a large number of deaths involving young people. The drug can cause sudden death in a number of ways, such as overheating leading to convulsions and collapse, and strokes caused by the formation of blood clots.

5. **False** – Between a quarter and a third of all the recorded solvent deaths each year in the UK are of young people who have no previous history of use. Solvents have a real potential to cause sudden death on first time use. The most common solvent currently

being misused is liquid petroleum gas (LPG), which is found in pressurised canisters for cooking, or used as heating or as a lighter fuel, and as the propellant in most aerosols. The solvent is usually squirted directly into the throat, and can cause sudden death in two ways. The release of the pressure causes a profound drop in temperature, and causes the tissues of the throat and larynx to swell, leading to asphyxiation. LPG can also lead to the over-production of the hormone adrenaline, which can lead to heart failure.

6. **True** – Using two drugs of a similar nature, such as two stimulants or depressants, can lead to overdose. Mixing drugs of differing natures can lead to unpredictable and often dangerous results.

7. **False** – Generally, males use drugs more commonly and in larger quantities than females. This picture is slowly changing, however, with an increasing number of females taking to drug use. They are still outnumbered by the male users but are increasing in number at a faster rate.

8. **True** – Many users report that they become involved in drug use in order to enhance their image with their peers. The image that such use has for some young people is of someone who is 'cool', 'smart', 'hard', 'in fashion' and so on. It needs to be pointed out, however, that many other young people view drug use as foolish and 'uncool'. Drug users will often provoke the opposite reaction to the one that they are seeking from their peers.

9. **False** – A person would need a good level of knowledge of fungi to positively identify members of the magic mushroom group when seen fresh. Once they have been dried, it would require the services of a laboratory to correctly identify them. Many of the problems caused by magic mushrooms occur when people use the wrong varieties, some of which are highly toxic.

10. **True** – Recent research has shown that young people who smoke tobacco are approximately four times more likely to become involved in taking illegal drugs. The reason is quite simple, for most young people have their first experience of illegal drugs with cannabis in a smoking form. It is much easier to say yes to an offer of cannabis in this form if you are already a smoker of cigarettes, since a smoker's body is already accustomed to accept the act of smoking; a non-smoker is unlikely to make his/her first smoking experience one of using cannabis.

11. **True** – Addiction or dependence, either physical or psychological, can develop to any drug with regular use by any method.

12. **True** – Tolerance develops to all drugs with regular use, meaning that the user requires increasing amounts of the drug to achieve a certain level of effect.

13. **False** – The act of injecting brings with it many problems. Using injecting equipment that has already been used by others exposes the user to any infections that the previous users may have. Infections such as HIV, hepatitis B and C, septicemia and gonorrhoea, can be contracted in this way. Injecting impure drugs that contain undissolved solids can block small blood vessels, potentially leading to gangrene. Injection sites frequently become infected and abscesses are common. If a drug is injected directly into the blood system it reaches the central nervous system within seconds. Once injected it cannot be removed and any overdosing is difficult to counter. Drugs taken orally can often be pumped or washed from the stomach, or vomited spontaneously.

14. **False** – Amphetamine (speed) use carries many physical risks and problems. Amphetamine is a powerful stimulant that leads to an increase in blood pressure, heart rate and body temperature. Any of these can lead to strokes or heart failure. Amphetamine is also a powerful appetite suppressant and disrupter of sleep patterns, and its use can lead to extreme weight loss and chronic insomnia. These two together can lead to a loss of body condition and a reduction in the efficiency of the body's immune system.

    Amphetamine use carries a very real risk of serious and often permanent damage to psychiatric health. Many users become depressed and anxious after using the drug for only a short time. Longer use can lead to paranoia, delusions and psychosis. Often these illnesses require in-patient treatment in psychiatric hospitals and can prove difficult if not impossible to cure.

15. **True** – No one starts to use illegal drugs in order to have a bad time, every one starts with the idea that they will have a good time or perhaps that drug use will mask unpleasant things in their lives. It has to be stated, however, that many users find that they have a very bad time indeed. Their entire lives can become totally dominated by their drug use, with dire consequences. A true friend would never encourage anyone to become involved in such a nightmare. It is a sad fact that the vast majority of young people who use drugs are introduced to them, and indeed even supplied, by a close friend. This may be because the friend is also a user and will be keen to get others involved to make him/herself feel better about his/her own use.

16. **True** – In the sense that the possession of illegal drugs in an illegal act and as such makes everyone who uses such drugs a criminal. Drug use is extremely common, indeed almost normal, amongst people involved in crimes of dishonesty, but such use is not confined to these types of people. Drug use is no respector of race, social background, gender, academic ability or financial position.

There is no such person as a typical drug user, for it can happen to anyone.

17. **True** – Many of the drugs prescribed by doctors have the potential to cause addiction, either physical or psychological. This is particularly true of tranquillisers, painkillers and sleeping tablets, and there are many thousands of people in the UK who are addicted to such products as a result of unwise prescribing. Doctors are now very aware of the addictive properties of some prescribed drugs and take great care to prevent their patients becoming addicted to them.

18. **True** – The sniffing of solvents will lead to rapid intoxication. Continued use can then lead on to loss of control over the user's bladder and bowels.

19. **False** – Thousands of people die each year as a direct result of becoming intoxicated with alcohol. Many of these deaths are those of young people. A person who is intoxicated can easily become involved in a reckless act that can lead to a serious accident. These accidents can place innocent bystanders in mortal danger as well as the intoxicated person. Besides the risk of accidents, an intoxicated person can become involved in criminal acts or unsafe sex, or simply make a complete and deeply embarrassing fool of him/herself.

20. (a) **True** – It is easy for a person whose judgement has been affected by their drug use to become involved in unprotected sex. This could easily lead to an unplanned pregnancy or even to a sexually transmitted disease.

    (b) **True** – Many street drugs can be purchased in small quantities at a low price. Once tolerance and addiction have been established, however, drug use can become very expensive. A common way of paying for such drug use is by becoming involved in crime. This will commonly be either in the form of drug dealing or theft, often accompanied by violence. It has been estimated that some 70 per cent of the crime committed in the UK is drug-related.

    (c) **True** – Drugs are easily obtained on credit and a considerable debt can quickly be built up. This places the debtor firmly in the control of the drug supplier. The debtor may be required to carry out a whole range of criminal acts to clear off the debt or may be subjected to a great deal of personal violence.

    (d) **True** – In order to finance an established drug habit, some users, both male and female, may turn to prostitution. This places them at grave risk of violence and of becoming infected with HIV or other sexually transmitted diseases.

(e) **True** – Many schools will enforce a policy of permanent exclusion for any involvement in drugs. This can have a seriously damaging effect on education and long-term career prospects.

Follow-up exercises

The quiz will have raised many issues connected with drug use. Any of these can be followed up with discussions, research projects, essay writing or in any other way that the leader sees as being appropriate and useful.

TRUE   FALSE

1.   Dope, marijuana, grass and canna-
     bis are different drugs.

2.   Medical drugs are often sold to
     young people as ecstasy.

3.   Street drugs are usually sold mixed
     with other substances.

4.   Ecstasy can cause mental health
     problems.

5.   Solvent sniffing has never killed
     anyone first time.

6.   Mixing different drugs can be espe-
     cially dangerous.

7.   Girls use drugs more than boys.

8.   Some people use drugs to look
     tough.

9.   It's easy to identify magic mush-
     rooms from other kinds.

10. Smoking cigarettes can lead to the
     use of other drugs.

11. Regular use of any drug can lead to
     addiction.

TRUE   FALSE

12. If a drug is used regularly the effect reduces unless the amount is increased.

13. Injecting is no more dangerous than any other way of using drugs.

14. Amphetamine (speed) is a safe drug for recreational use.

15. A good friend will not encourage you to take drugs.

16. All people who use illegal drugs are criminals.

17. Some people become hooked on certain drugs prescribed by doctors.

18. Solvent use can make you lose control of your bladder.

19. Getting drunk on alcohol never hurt anyone.

20. Drug use can lead to:

    (a) pregnancy;
    (b) crime;
    (c) debt;
    (d) prostitution;
    (e) exclusion from school.

Can You Help Me Please?

Suggested age: 13+

Outline

An exercise to place the participants in situations where they are required to respond to others who are appealing for their help in dealing with a drug-related situation.

Purpose and expected outcome

- To encourage participants to consider the difficulties encountered by drug users and others around them who are affected.

- To encourage participants to consider all of the aspects of a drug situation and to look at ways in which those who are adversely affected by it can be helped.

- To discover what resources are available to help people with a drug-related problem.

- To encourage individual responsibility over drug decisions.

- To challenge attitudes to drug use. To reinforce drug prevention messages.

Method

The teacher or leader should briefly explain the exercise and then split the class up into groups of four or five. Each group should be given a copy of one of the letters. It may be that with large classes more than one group will have the same letter to work with. Each group is instructed to consider the letter in detail and to prepare an answer that gives, to the best of its ability, advice that will enable the writer to resolve the situation in a positive manner. After sufficient time has elapsed for discussion, each group is asked to report back to the rest of the class the results of its discussions. This report can take the form of reading out a response letter that the group have composed or, more simply, stating the points that have been considered. The rest of the class should be encouraged to ask questions, to challenge any of the advice given, and to offer suggestions of their own.

Notes for teacher or group leader

It is important that the groups consider as many aspects as possible of the problems detailed in the letters, and in particular, how the actions of any one of the characters involved in the situation can affect those around them. An appendix is provided which lists agencies that offer help and advice to people involved in drug-related situations. Participants may like to find out whether there are more locally based services in their area.

Follow-up exercises

The letters can be set as an individual exercise with participants giving verbal or written answers. The class can be instructed to carry out research and draw up a list of help lines and agencies in their locality. The class can examine advice columns in newspapers and magazines, particularly those aimed at young readers, and discuss the level and quality of advice given.

Meadowlands
Orchard Lane
Tynesworth

Dear Lisa

I am 14, my parents are divorced and I live with my mum. Three months ago my mum's boyfriend, Tommy, came to live with us. I don't get on with him, he always seems to be finding fault with me and picking on me. Since he moved in he has begun to sell drugs to people who call at the back door. He tries to hide it, but I have seen the stuff in my mum's room. I don't like drugs and am afraid that my mum will get into trouble with the police. If I tell my dad what's happening he will go crazy, he'd probably kill Tommy. What can I do, should I tell my dad, or is there anything else I can do? I'm desperate, please help.

Richard

15 Park Drive
Willowbend
Cleveland

Dear John

My mate and I are both 14 and go to the same school. There is a group of boys in our year who throw their weight around a lot. They pick on lots of people but especially on us. We get called all sorts of names because we both go to scouts. I think scouts is great, next month we are going climbing in the Brecon Beacons in Wales. The thing is, my mate says that he is getting fed up with all the name calling at school and is going to give up scouts and try and get on the good side of this other group by being more like them. He says 'if you can't beat them you might as well join them'. This crowd seem to spend most of their time just hanging around and causing trouble, I have heard that they all use cannabis and speed and try other things. I don't want my mate getting into that. What shall I do — please help.

Dave

The Coach House
Mill Cross Lane
Sayerstown

Dear Clara

I am nearly 14 and go out with a really great boyfriend called Glen.
He is 17 and used to go to our school. He used to get in a lot of
trouble because the teachers picked on him. He can't get the sort
of job he wants and so he stays in bed all morning. He really loves
me and treats me like an adult. He says that we should have sex
because that would mean that we really love each other. I know he
smokes a bit of dope and he lets me have a puff sometimes,
although I don't like him using it because he gets moody afterwards.
He keeps asking me to lend him money and has even said I could
nick money from my dad's shop for him. I really love him but I'm not
sure what I should do. What do you think?

Maureen

30 Bells Crescent
Bournebrook
Testerton

Dear Brett

Please help me, I am going crazy and am really confused. I am just 14 and have a brother who's 16. He sniffs lighter gas all the time and gets right out of his head. He spends all of his money on cans of gas and sits up in the subway near our house with his mates every evening and sniffs it. He sprays it straight in his mouth. I heard that it is dangerous. I tried to tell him but he told me to mind my own business and hit me in the face. He's always in trouble at school and at home. We live with my dad since my mum left and I don't think my dad knows, it would kill him; he tries so hard to be both mum and dad to us. Should I tell him about my brother? What should I do? Is it dangerous like they say?

Glenda

The Bell House
Church Close
Tensingbury

Dear Gary

I really need your help. There is no one else I can turn to and if you can't help I don't know what I'm going to do. I'm 15 and an only child and the thing is, over the past three months I've got into sniffing aerosols. It started as a dare with some of my mates at a party one night. We all had a go and got out of our heads. I had tried it again the next night at home and really liked it . Anyway now I'm getting through several aerosols a day. My parents are out at work during the day and go out most evenings so I have been able to hide it from them. I'm spending a lot of money on it now and have to steal some of it from home to buy enough cans. My parents would kill me if they found out. I think I need help, I feel really rough most of the time and can't stop. I feel so rough some mornings that I don't get to school and I think that my parents will find out soon. What shall I do? Please help.

Rory

27 Kings Road
Millsborough

Dear Francis

I am in year ten at my school and there is a girl in my year who is
selling drugs at school. She gets them from her older mates and
sells them to other kids. She even sells them to much younger kids. I
don't think she pushes them on anyone but she just lets it get
around that she has them if anyone wants them. I'm not too sure
but she seems to have all sorts of drugs, even hard ones, for sale. I
don't like what she is doing but I don't want anyone to think that I'm
a sneak or a dobber so I couldn't tell a teacher. What should I do, I'm
really worried about it.

Dean

EXERCISE 8

What About Us ?

Suggested age: 13+

Outline

An exercise to encourage participants to consider who in society is affected by others who use drugs, and to examine the degree and seriousness of that effect.

Purpose and expected outcome

- To increase participants' awareness and understanding that drug use, either their own or that of others, not only affects the user, but has wider implications and effects for those around them.
- To encourage participants to consider the effects that drug taking has on society as a whole.
- To encourage individual responsibility over drug decisions.
- To challenge attitudes to drug use.
- To reinforce drug prevention messages.

Method

The teacher or group leader should briefly outline the exercise and split the class into small groups. The blank target work sheets should then be distributed and participants instructed to write in the column the names of those individuals or groups that are, in their opinion, affected by someone else's drug use. They should then be told to write the number of the person or group that they consider is most affected close to the bullseye of the target, and those less affected further away. After sufficient time has elapsed for this part of the exercise each group should report back to the rest of the class its list and order of importance. The teacher can transfer this list to the board or perhaps to the projected image of the bullseye. Other members of the class should be encouraged to question the inclusion of particular individuals or groups of persons on any list, and also the positioning. Once all of the groups have reported back it may be possible to draw up a class list showing where there are areas of agreement. The suggested check-list can be used as an example, and a general discussion held on the way in which those on it or the lists produced by the class, are affected by drug use; and what the possible consequences of those effects might be.

Notes for teacher or group leader

The class can be provided with examples from the suggested list to start them off, if that is considered necessary. They should be encouraged to think of all of the possibilities and not to restrict their thinking just to their immediate circle of family, friends and associates.

Follow-up exercises

Participants could enter into the role of one of those identified as being affected by someone else's drug use, and look closely at the ways in which they personally would be affected, and the consequences arising from such effects.

THOSE AFFECTED BY DRUG USE

Make a list, in any order, of those whom you think can be affected by a person's drug use. Write the item number in the position on the target that you think is appropiate, placing those most affected closest to the centre.

USER

LIST

1.
2.
3.
4.
5.
6.
7.
8.
9.
10.
11.
12.
13.
14.
15.
16.
17.
18.
19.
20.

THOSE AFFECTED BY DRUG USE

Make a list, in any order, of those whom you think can be affected by a person's drug use. Write the item number in the position on the target that you think is appropiate, placing those most affected closest to the centre.

CHECK LIST

1. Partner/parents
2. Children
3. Brothers and sisters
4. Family
5. Close friends
6. School/college
7. Neighbours
8. Community
9. Victims of crime
10. Colleagues
11. Employees
12. Employers
13. Tax payers
14. Health service
15. Street cleaners
16. Insurers
17. Police
18. Courts
19. Social services
20. Prisons

USER

Drug Diamond Nine

Suggested age: 12 +

Outline

An exercise to encourage participants to examine pressures, temptations and reasons that lead young people to start or to continue using drugs. It also looks at the corresponding pressures, temptations and reasons that prevent many young people from using drugs, or that encourage current users to stop.

Purpose and expected outcome

- To enable the examination of issues that affect drug use decisions.
- To place such issues in order of their importance.
- To encourage participants to consider the drug decisions of others.
- To challenge attitudes to drug use.
- To reinforce drug prevention messages.

Method

The worksheets should be copied and cut up to produce sufficient sets for small groupwork. If it is intended that the sets should be used repeatedly they can be laminated. The teacher or group leader should briefly outline the purpose of the exercise, and split the class up into small groups. The cards that deal with reasons to start or continue drug use should be distributed, one set to each group. Groups should be asked to consider the reasons printed on each card and to select nine of them that, in their opinion, represent the most powerful pressures, temptations or reasons for a young person to start drug use or for an existing user to continue. Each set includes a blank card that can be used by the group to include a reason that it feels has been omitted. Having selected nine cards the group should then arrange them in the 'diamond nine' layout, as shown.

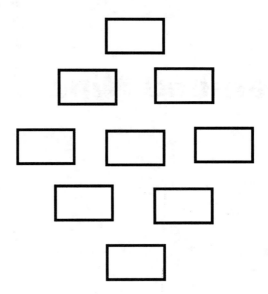

The top position should be occupied by the card that, in the opinion of the group, contains the most important and powerful reason to start or continue drug use. The two positions in the second row should be occupied by the cards that contain the next most important or powerful reasons, the middle row the three next most important and so on, until the bottom position is filled by the card that contains the least important reason. When sufficient time has elapsed for each group to arrange its cards in a 'diamond nine', it should report its choice and placings back to the rest of the class. A simple scoring system can be used to arrive at a common 'diamond nine'. The card placed at the top by any group should be awarded one point, cards placed in the second row two points and so on down to the bottom card which should be awarded five points. Cards not selected for inclusion in any group's 'diamond nine' should be awarded six points. When all of the groups have reported back, the points can be added up to produce a common placings lists. The card that scores the lowest number of points should be placed at the top, the next two in the second row, and so on until the common 'diamond nine' is complete. The two cards that have the highest scores are left out. The teacher can then ask each group why it chose to place a particular card where it did. Groups can also be asked to justify leaving out certain cards or placing them in a lower position. General discussion can then take place. The exercise involving cards containing pressures, temptations and reasons for young people not to start drug use, or for existing users to stop their drug use, can be used in exactly the same way. This can be used immediately following the previous 'diamond nine' exercise or on a separate occasion.

Notes for teacher or group leader

There are no entirely right or wrong answers in this exercise. It is an opportunity for participants to discuss their views and, having come to an agreement, indicate their reasoning. Providing the group has given sufficient thought to the placings and is prepared to explain its reasoning, then any placing order is valid. If a group is unable to agree a particular placing, then a simple vote may resolve the dispute. When a dispute is not resolved by voting, then a separate minority placing order may be accepted. Every effort, however, should be taken to achieve agreement.

Follow-up exercises

Creating a set of reasons for becoming involved in other forms of risk taking behaviour, e.g. climbing, canoeing, surfing, theft, vandalism and so on. Looking at how such pressures, temptations and reasons exert their influence over young people.

REASONS TO START OR CONTINUE DRUG USE

	TO BE LIKE EVERYONE ELSE
PRESSURE FROM FRIENDS	**THE EXCITEMENT OF RISK TAKING**
EXPERIMENTING OUT OF CURIOSITY	**THE THRILL OF DOING SOMETHING ILLEGAL**
TO JOIN IN WITH A GROUP	**YOU ONLY GET A CAUTION IF YOU GET CAUGHT**
TO HAVE A GOOD TIME	**EVERYONE IS DOING IT**
BECAUSE JUST TRYING THEM NEVER HURT ANYONE	**TO HELP FORGET PROBLEMS**

REASONS TO STOP OR NOT TO START DRUG USE

	THE DEATH OF A FRIEND
GETTING CAUGHT BY THE POLICE	**A GIRL/BOY FRIEND WHO DISAPPROVES**
A BAD PERSONAL DRUGS EXPERIENCE	**PARENTS FINDING OUT**
DISAPPROVAL OF FRIENDS	**FINANCIAL COST**
FEAR OF ADDICTION	**HEALTH RISKS**
RISK TO EDUCATION AND CAREER	**MEDIA REPORTS OF DRUG USE**

Benefits and Drawbacks

Suggested age: 13+

Outline

An exercise to enable participants to consider the benefits and drawbacks of illegal drugs and medicines or prescription drugs and to compare the two.

Purpose and expected outcome

- To encourage the consideration of potential problems associated with illegal drug use.
- To increase the participants' understanding of the possible outcomes of drug use.
- To encourage individual responsibility over drug decisions.
- To challenge attitudes to drug use.
- To reinforce drug prevention messages.

Method

The teacher or group leader should briefly outline the exercise and then split the class into small groups. The groups are issued with the blank worksheets and are then asked to consider all of the possible benefits and drawbacks that can be associated with the use of illegal drugs, and with medicines and pre-scribed drugs. The groups should be encouraged to think deeply about the subject, and to consider as many issues as possible, drawing up lists on the respective worksheets. After sufficient time has been allowed, each group should report back to the rest of the class the issues on the lists. Groups can be restricted to a small number of issues so that each can make a contribution. The suggested issues can be drawn up as a class list on the board. When each group has made its contribution, a general discussion of the points raised and their importance can follow. The class should then be asked to rearrange the issues in order of importance.

Notes for teacher or group leader

A check-list is provided that can be used to add extra items into the lists produced by the groups. The exercise can be carried out as an individual activity with each participant being issued with a blank work sheet or, alternatively, the blank worksheets can be produced as overhead transparencies and projected onto a white board. The whole class can then contribute while the teacher enters the suggested items onto the projected worksheets.

Follow-up exercises

Pupils can be asked to collect newspaper reports of incidents where either illegal or legal drugs have caused problems. Pupils can be asked to collect instruction leaflets from various medicines and prescribed drugs, and then to compare the amount of information that is provided by such leaflets with the amount of good factual information that is made available by suppliers of illegal drugs.

ILLEGAL DRUGS

Benefits

Drawbacks

ILLEGAL DRUGS

Benefits	Drawbacks
Readily available	No quality control
May give desired effect	Uncertain strength
No prescription needed	High cost
To some they may appear 'cool'	Mixed with other substances
	Not medically tested
	No specified dose
	May lead to criminal charge
	Addiction
	Tolerance
	Withdrawal symptoms
	Many 'snidey' drugs
	Unpredictable effects, even after previous use
	Supply may be cut off
	No medical supervision
	Danger of overdose
	If injected, can lead to other health problems
	No redress if dissatisfied

MEDICINES AND PRESCRIBED DRUGS

93

Benefits   **Drawbacks**

MEDICINES AND PRESCRIBED DRUGS

Benefits	Drawbacks
Known strength	Need to consult a doctor
Medically tested	
Known and predictable effects	
Low cost to user	
No adulterants	
Constant supply	
Supervised use	
Not usually injected	
No 'snideys'	
No legal risks if prescribed for user	
Redress available for poor quality or bad effects	
No involvement in crime	

Scenarios

Suggested age: 14 +

Outline

An exercise to encourage participants to look at what other options are available to people who are facing difficulties or pressures in their lives, rather than the use of drugs.

Purpose and expected outcome

- To enable participants to explore possible ways of avoiding dangerous situations.
- To encourage participants to examine the sources of help that are available to those experiencing difficulties.
- To encourage individual responsibility over drug decisions.
- To challenge attitudes to drug use.
- To reinforce drug prevention messages.

Method

The teacher or group leader should briefly outline the exercise and split the class into small groups. Each group should be issued with a copy of one of the scenarios and should then be asked to discuss the scenario and to answer the following questions:

1. How could the person in the scenario have avoided getting into the particular situation?
2. Where could he/she have gone for help or advice?

3. What are the possible further problems that he/she might face if the situation does not change?

4. Now that he/she is in the situation, what can he/she do to change it?

5. Where might he/she go to seek help and advice ?

The teacher should allow sufficient time for the group to consider all of the possibilities in the situation, and then ask it to report back to the rest of class the various points that it has discussed, and the solutions that it proposes. The rest of the class can comment upon the points raised and the suggested solutions.

Notes for teacher or group leader

The session leader will need to be aware that some of the participants may be in personal circumstances that are closely similar to those in the scenarios, and will need to be sensitive to this. It may be advisable to remove a particular scenario if this is felt to be too 'close to home' for any member of the class.

This exercise can be used as an individual exercise, with pupils being asked to consider and answer one or a number of scenarios, verbally or in writing. As an alternative the teacher can read one of the scenarios to the class and then hold a general discussion on the points that it raises, and take suggested answers from the class to the questions posed earlier.

A list of agencies that might be able to offer help and advice is given as an appendix to this book.

Follow-up exercises

Pupils can be asked to research and draw up a list of national or local helping agencies that offer advice in these types of situations.

Pupils can be asked to collect newspaper reports of real life drug-related situations, and to discuss them in the same way as they have discussed the scenarios.

SCENARIO 1

Teresa is a young mother of 24. Her husband, Richard, works away, sending money home from time to time. Teresa cannot manage on the money she receives, especially as she has three young children who constantly need new clothes, shoes, etc. She feels that she cannot talk to her husband, and gets no support from her family. She is quite shy and hasn't really made friends with anybody in the village where she lives. She has taken to drinking alcohol to ease her anxiety, but this is eating into her inadequate budget. She receives a valium prescription from her doctor, but uses more than the stated dose. As she feels depressed, she has been considering using street speed as she did when she was 18, since this seemed to lift her mood.

SCENARIO 2

Ben is 11 and has just started secondary school. He is small for his age and gets picked on by older boys who push him around and steal his belongings. He is too frightened to tell anybody about this, especially his father who is very strict, and he feels that it might worry his mother too much. In order to help him cope with all the pressure, Ben sniffs lighter fuel from a plastic bag under a bridge by the local canal, usually straight after school.

SCENARIO 3

Gavin is 16 and lives with his parents. Recently his first real girlfriend, Sandra, left him for one of his friends, since when he has become more and more depressed and withdrawn. He has become friendly with another boy who supplies him with speed and LSD, which Gavin uses daily to try and get on with his life. Although he feels OK when he is using the drugs, he feels much worse when the effects wear off. He has begun to shoplift and to steal money from home in order to pay for his new habit. His homework is also suffering, and recently he was suspended for a week for swearing at a teacher.

SCENARIO 4

Tara is 18 and attends college. She made friends with a crowd who go clubbing at weekends and quickly got into using ecstasy. She now has a tolerance to the drug and is using eight tablets or capsules every weekend, which she told her dealer is costing her too much. He suggested that she might start earning some money by supplying the drug to other friends of hers, which she did. Unfortunately, she was caught last week by the police and will have to go to court charged with supplying. Her parents have been told and are threatening to throw her out of their home and the college have also found out and may expel her.

SCENARIO 5

Michael is 35 and gets very agitated and worried about his new job, which he finds too much for him. At the end of the day he can't wait to get home, but once there he just worries about the next day. He is not sleeping very well and has started to smoke cannabis in the evening to help him relax and to sleep. In the morning he is not in a fit state to drive to work, let alone do his job. He has started to make mistakes in his work and colleagues have begun to make comments about it.

SCENARIO 6

Debbie is 20 and lives alone. Since she lost her job she has started to use heroin and, because of developing tolerance and in order to get the greatest effect from it, has started injecting. She does not like injecting but sees little choice. Her habit has become very expensive, and she now works as a prostitute in order to pay for it. Many of her clients offer her extra money to have sex without using a condom and she often agrees.

SCENARIO 7

Danny is just 18 and lives with his aunt. His parents split up two years ago. He has a job and goes out with friends most weekends to dances and raves where he uses LSD and ecstasy and sometimes speed. Lately he has been experiencing some strange feelings and thoughts, and thinks that he may have done some permanent damage to his brain. This, he believes, is backed up by friends of his who say that he has 'lost it', and that he is 'off his head'. Sometimes he hears voices and feels that he is being watched. He doesn't know what to do. He would like to stop using the drugs, but he thinks that he can't have a good time without using them.

SCENARIO 8

Lisa recently lost her job at the bank for constantly turning up late with no explanation. She feels that she cannot tell her father with whom she lives. Her mother left home some years before. She carries on a pretence of going to work by leaving home at the same time every morning. Her father knows that she smokes cannabis, but doesn't really mind as long as she keeps her job. She has now taken to smoking small amounts of heroin during the day, to pass the time and to take away her bad feelings. She gets the heroin from an old school friend, who is allowing her credit until she can pay him.

SCENARIO 9

Mandy is 21 and currently lives with her boyfriend, Pete, on a travellers' site. They both use speed and heroin, which they inject, and smoke cannabis. Mandy knows that she is three months pregnant but has not told Pete. She does not know what she wants to do about the pregnancy and is worried about the possible damage that her drug use may be doing to her baby.

SCENARIO 10

Two 14-year-old boys have been taken to hospital from school, as they both became very ill during the lunch break. Nobody seems to know why, but it is believed that they were seen buying some tablets from an older boy who told them that these tablets were a new type of ecstasy.

SCENARIO 11

Steve is 14 and lives at home with his parents and two younger brothers. His parents are going through a difficult patch in their marriage and have spoken of divorce. Steve started using lighter gas with some of his friends in the evenings. They all sit in the subway near the shops and have been spraying the gas directly into their mouths. Recently, one of his friends was very ill after using the gas and taken to hospital. The others have all stopped using since then but Steve finds that he can't. He has tried talking to some other friends at school about it but they just told him not to be stupid and to pack it up.

SCENARIO 12

Martin is 12 and lives in a children's home. He still sees his mother occasionally but has never seen his father. His mother drinks a lot and can't look after him. He finds it very difficult to make friends with the other children in the home and at school. He spends most of his time on his own and is very lonely and unhappy. Recently, a new boy has moved into the home and seems to like Martin. He spends a lot of time with Martin and makes him laugh. He smokes cannabis and talks of using speed and LSD. He says Martin should use them as well as they would make him feel better. Martin is afraid of what might happen but does not want to upset his new friend.

In My View

Suggested age: 14 +

Outline

An exercise to enable participants to take the role of a person involved in a situation brought about by someone else's drug use, and to consider the options open to such a person.

Purpose and expected outcome

- To encourage consideration of the problems caused to other people involved with and around the drug user.
- To build understanding of how a person's drug use affects others.
- To encourage individual responsibility over drug decisions.
- To challenge attitudes to drug use.
- To reinforce drug prevention messages.

Method

The teacher or group leader should briefly outline the exercise and then split the class into small groups. Copies of the scenarios in exercise 11 should be distributed, one to each group. Each group should then be issued with one of the work sheets from this exercise. The group is asked to take on the role of the person or group named in the centre of this worksheet and consider the scenario from that viewpoint. The group should discuss the situation and then attempt to answer the four questions shown on the worksheet, viz: How would you feel? Whom should you tell? What could you do? What problems will you face? Participants should be encouraged to look at all possibilities that might flow from their chosen course of action, and then to consider any alternative courses of action. After sufficient time for discussion, each group should be asked to report back to the rest of their class, who should be encouraged to comment on the points raised and the courses of action suggested. The worksheets can then be swapped between groups, allowing each of them to consider the same scenario from the perspective of another person, or the scenarios themselves can be swapped. This process can be repeated as many times as the teacher wishes.

Notes for teacher or group leader

As in exercise 11, the teacher leading the session will need to be aware that some of the participants may be in personal circumstances that are closely similar to those in the scenarios, and should be sensitive to them. It may be advisable to remove a particular scenario if this is felt to be too 'close to home' for any member of the class.

The exercise can also be used on an individual basis or carried out with the class as a whole. It could also be set as a written exercise.

A list of helping agencies is provided as an appendix to this book.

Follow-up exercises

Selected scenarios could be acted out with participants being given the opportunity of taking different roles so that they can explore some of the feelings such persons might experience in situations of this nature.

1.

2.

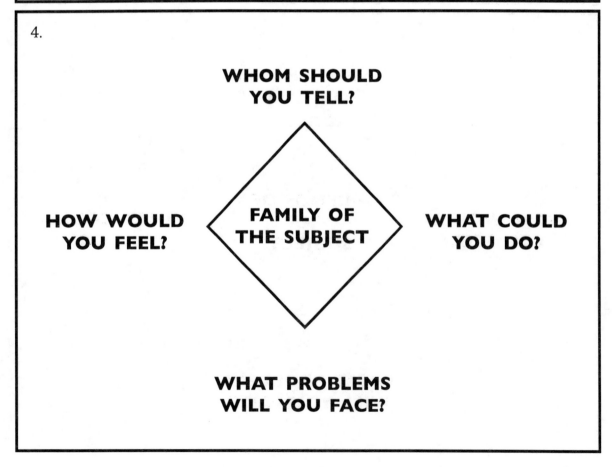

3.

WHOM SHOULD
YOU TELL?

HOW WOULD
YOU FEEL?

PARTNER OF
THE SUBJECT

WHAT COULD
YOU DO?

WHAT PROBLEMS
WILL YOU FACE?

4.

WHOM SHOULD
YOU TELL?

HOW WOULD
YOU FEEL?

FAMILY OF
THE SUBJECT

WHAT COULD
YOU DO?

WHAT PROBLEMS
WILL YOU FACE?

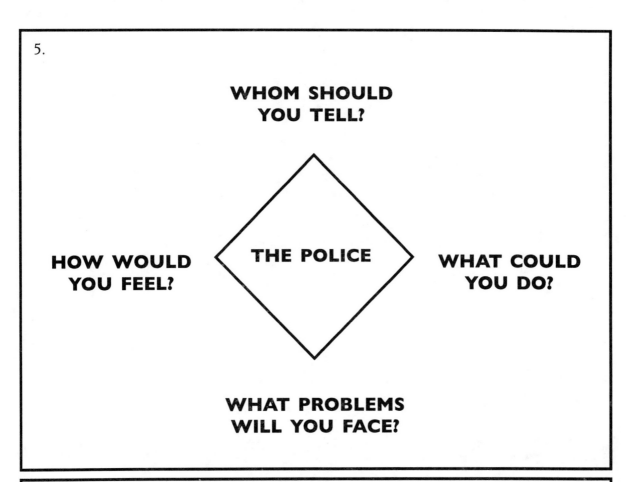

5.

WHOM SHOULD
YOU TELL?

HOW WOULD
YOU FEEL?

THE POLICE

WHAT COULD
YOU DO?

WHAT PROBLEMS
WILL YOU FACE?

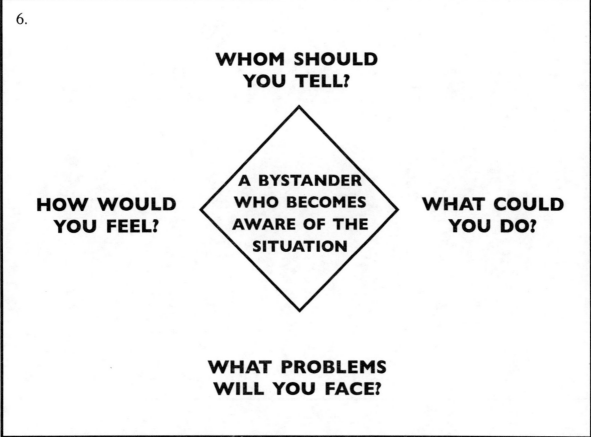

6.

WHOM SHOULD
YOU TELL?

HOW WOULD
YOU FEEL?

A BYSTANDER
WHO BECOMES
AWARE OF THE
SITUATION

WHAT COULD
YOU DO?

WHAT PROBLEMS
WILL YOU FACE?

EXERCISE 13

Law and Penalties

Suggested age: 13+

Outline

A multi-choice format quiz that enables participants to explore their knowledge of the law as it applies to the use of illegal drugs.

Purpose and expected outcome

- To enable participants to improve their knowledge and understanding of drug laws.
- To clarify some of the myths that surround the law in relation to drug use.
- To prompt discussion of the relevance of the drug laws.
- To encourage individual responsibility over drug decisions.
- To challenge attitudes to drug use.
- To reinforce drug prevention messages.

Method

The quiz sheets contain 25 questions designed to be suitable for young people aged 13 years and above. Each question is accompanied by a choice of answers, only one of which is correct.

It should be explained to the participants that the purpose of the quiz is not to examine their level of knowledge about drug laws, but rather to enable them to check out the accuracy or otherwise of the knowledge that they already have, and to add useful and balanced information.

The quiz sheets should be copied and handed out to the participants and time allowed for them to answer the questions. The teacher or leader should then go through the answers using the following guidance notes. Many of the questions will prompt discussion of associated drug issues. This is intended and should be encouraged.

Participants should correct their sheets in line with the given answers and keep them for future reference.

Notes for teacher or group leader

CORRECT ANSWERS:

1. Cannabis is a class B drug and possession of it for personal use is punishable on indictment by a term of imprisonment not exceeding **five years**. It is highly unlikely that anyone would receive a sentence of this length for possession of small quantities for personal use. Most juveniles who are found in possession of small amounts of cannabis will receive an official police caution. It has become much less common in recent times for people who have received a drug caution to be given further cautions should they be arrested again for possession of drugs. Subsequent appearances at court for cannabis possession can and often do lead to terms of imprisonment.

2. Generally speaking, a person **cannot** be charged with possession of a drug once it has been taken into the body. It is worth noting that items such as cannabis cigarette butts, bhongs (cannabis water-pipes), paper wraps, needles and syringes and scales, will normally contain traces of the drug that they have been used with, and provide enough evidence on which to base a possession charge.

3. Passing a cannabis cigarette to a friend for them to share, most certainly **can** and does lead to charges of supplying the drug. A charge of supplying does not require that any money or goods have been exchanged, for the charge is supplying, not selling, and sharing any drug with someone else is considered to be an act of supplying. The maximum penalty for supplying cannabis is 14 years' imprisonment, an unlimited fine and the seizure of all drug-related assets.

4. The active drugs in most varieties of 'magic' or hallucinogenic mushrooms are psilocybin and psilocin. Both of these substances are **class A** drugs. The possession of fresh raw magic mushrooms is not an offence under the drug legislation: it requires some act of preparing the mushrooms for consumption to activate the law. Slicing, crushing, cooking, drying or any other act of preparation would make the offender liable to penalties under class A of the legislation. (See law and penalties sheet on page 146 for a complete

breakdown of these offences.) It is worth noting that although the picking of magic mushrooms may not be an offence under the drug laws, it can be considered to be theft under the Theft Act if permission to pick has not been given by the owner of the land upon which the mushrooms are found. It is also an offence under various pieces of environmental legislation to pick magic mushrooms for sale to others, as most species of magic mushrooms are protected fungi.

5. Using anabolic steroids is **not** a criminal offence. It is an offence under the Medicines Act for an unlicensed person to supply them to someone else.

6. It is **legal** for a person under the age of 16 to buy solvents. The Intoxicating Substance Supply Act makes it an offence for a person to supply a solvent product to a person apparently under the age of 18 years, if they have reason to suspect that the person is going to use the solvents for intoxication.

7. Selling fake ecstasy tablets is **not** an offence under the drug laws. Drug customers are not protected under any consumer legislation. If the seller falsely stated that they were ecstasy, a charge of deception under the Theft Act might be possible.

8. Possessing needles or syringes is **not** an offence.

9. Parents or any other persons who allow premises over which they have control to be used for the smoking of cannabis **do** commit an offence, punishable on indictment by 14 years imprisonment.

10. You **can** be charged, sent to court, and indeed imprisoned on a first drug offence. It is common for people with no previous history of drug offences, who are found in possession of small amounts of drugs for personal use, to be cautioned by the police; but this is not automatic.

11. It **is** illegal to supply prescription only drugs to others. Some prescription drugs are controlled by the Misuse of Drugs Act and the rest by the Medicine Act. Both acts carry heavy penalties.

12. Drivers **can** and often are charged with the specific offence of driving on a road whilst unfit due to the use of drugs. Road traffic accidents caused by drivers affected by drugs are on the increase in the UK.

13. You **could** be charged with GBH if the resultant 'trip' experienced by the unwitting taker of the LSD led to them being harmed. You could also be charged with an offence of administering a poison to another person.

14. Supplying heroin, a class A drug, to another person is punishable on indictment by a maximum sentence of **life** imprisonment.

15. The courts **can** confiscate any assets in the possession of drug dealers if they are thought to have been acquired with profits from drug dealing.

16. Drugs have **not** been legalised in Holland. This applies to all drugs including cannabis. The government has decided to 'turn a blind eye' to the cultivation, possession and use of cannabis, but it remains an offence under Dutch law.

17. In the UK, doctors **can** prescribe pharmaceutical forms of heroin and amphetamine. No medical uses of cannabis are currently recognised and doctors **cannot** prescribe it.

18. Poppers (nitrites) **are** legal in the UK with the exception of amyl nitrite, which has recently been outlawed.

19. Dentists **may** use pharmaceutical forms of cocaine as a local anaesthetic although this is now rare.

20. You **can** be sent to prison for a drug offence whilst pregnant. The fact that a person is pregnant can be taken into consideration when fixing a penalty, but is not a bar to imprisonment.

21. Looking after someone else's drugs **is** an offence. A person doing this is guilty of possession.

22. A person finding an illegal drug **is** allowed to take possession of it to prevent its use. The finder must then dispose of the drug correctly as soon as is practicable. The normal way of disposing is to pass them to the police or to a community drug service.

23. If convicted of any drug offence you are very **likely** to be barred from entry or working in many foreign countries. Having a drug conviction can be a very serious impediment: the person concerned can find him/herself barred not only from many foreign countries but also from employment with many companies in the UK.

24. You **can** be charged with offences carried out under the influence of drugs. Acting under such influence is not an excuse and can lead to even heavier penalties being applied.

25. The cultivation of cannabis plants is punishable on indictment by a maximum of **14 years'** imprisonment.

Follow-up exercises

The quiz will have raised many issues connected with drug use and the law. Any of these can be followed up with discussions, debates, research projects or essay writing, or in any other way that the group leader sees as being appropriate and useful.

LAW AND PENALTIES

Put a circle around the correct answer.

1. Possession of cannabis for personal use can lead to a sentence of **two/five/seven/ten** years.

2. You **can/cannot** be charged with possession of a drug if it is in your bloodstream.

3. Passing a spliff (cannabis cigarette) to a friend for them to have a toke, or puff, of **can/cannot** be considered in law to be supplying the drug.

4. The drug in magic mushrooms is a class **A/B/C** drug.

5. Using anabolic steroids **is/is not** a criminal offence.

6. It is **legal/illegal** for a 16-year-old to purchase solvents.

7. Selling fake ecstasy tablets is/is not an offence under the drug laws.

8. Possessing needles and syringes for injecting drugs **is/is not** illegal.

9. If your parents allow you to smoke cannabis at home they **do/do not** commit a criminal offence.

10. You **can/cannot** be charged and sent to court for your first drugs offence.

11. It **is/is not** illegal to give prescription drugs to a friend.

12. Drivers **can/cannot** be prosecuted if they drive under the influence of drugs rather than alcohol.

LAW AND PENALTIES

Put a circle around the correct answer

13. You **could/could not** be charged with causing grievous bodily harm for putting LSD in someone's drink without them knowing.

14. Supplying heroin could lead to a prison sentence of **life/20/10** years.

15. Money made from the supply or manufacture of drugs **can/cannot** be confiscated by the courts.

16. Drugs **have/have not** been legalised in Holland.

17. In the UK, doctors **can/cannot** prescribe heroin/cannabis/amphetamine.

18. Poppers **are/are not** legal substances.

19. Dentists **may/may not** legally use cocaine on their patients.

20. You **can/cannot** be sent to prison for a drug offence if you are pregnant.

21. Looking after someone else's illegal drugs **is/is not** an offence.

22. A person finding illegal drugs **is/is not** allowed in law to take possession of them.

23. If convicted of a drug offence, you are **likely/unlikely** to be barred from entry into or working in many foreign countries.

24. You **can/cannot** be charged with any offence if it is carried out under the influence of drugs.

25. Growing cannabis plants can lead to a prison sentence of **2/5/7/10/12/14** years.

Jigsaw Drugs

Suggested age: 13 +

Outline

An exercise in which participants reassemble facts regarding particular drugs into an information poster.

Purpose and expected outcome

- To encourage participants to check out their knowledge about certain drugs.
- To give balanced information about drugs and their effects.
- To clarify some of the myths that surround drug use.
- To challenge attitudes to drug use.
- To reinforce drug prevention messages.

Method

The worksheets detail facts regarding a number of drugs or substances of misuse. The leader should copy the worksheets and then cut them up into their constituent parts. The boxes containing the drug name and its description should be cut out separately. The human figure should be cut into its two halves, one half containing the effects of the drug or substance, the other the problems linked with its use. Finally the two boxes detailing its method of use and its legal status should be cut out individually. These sections can be laminated if prolonged use is anticipated. This exercise is intended for use with a small group. The names of the 12 substances should be laid out in front of the group. The 12 descriptions are then dealt to the members of the group as in a card game. Taking turns each participant is then asked to fit one of their descriptions to its correct substance name. When all of the descriptions have been fitted correctly into place the participants are dealt the left sides of the human figure detailing the effects of the substances. As before the participants are asked to take turns fitting the sections under the correct name and description. This process is then repeated with the right-hand side of the human figure and the method of administration and legal status sections. The leader should ensure that each section is fitted in its correct place by referring to the worksheet originals. As each section is fitted into place the leader should draw the groups attention to any further points regarding the particular substance under consideration. The worksheets could also be produced as OHP slides for work with larger groups.

Notes for teacher or group leader

The purpose of this exercise is not to test participants' knowledge regarding individual drugs, but rather to allow them to explore and to increase their knowledge and to check out various beliefs and myths. Detailed information on each of the drugs and substances in this exercise is to be found in the drugs sections of *Understanding Drugs* by David Emmett and Graeme Nice, published by Jessica Kingsley Publishers (1995).

Follow-up exercises

Using the format and information in each work sheet to produce larger posters for class room display. This could be enhanced by using pictures of real people instead of the human figures. Particular drugs could be researched further, and a complete list of effects and problems created and added to the posters.

LSD

SMALL PAPER SQUARES WITH A DESIGN PRINTED ON THEM
VERY SMALL TABLETS OF VARIOUS COLOURS

EFFECTS

Visual, auditory and tactile hallucinations.

Can be pleasurable, neutral, unpleasant or nightmarish.

Out-of-body experiences.

PROBLEMS

Unpleasant or terrifying hallucinations.

Tolerance and habituation.

Flashbacks. Disorientation and potential for mental illness.

Accidents whilst hallucinating.

USUALLY TAKEN BY MOUTH

POSSESSION ILLEGAL CLASS A DRUG

CANNABIS

DRIED HERB-LIKE MIXTURE, PIECES OF RESIN
FROM BLACK TO LIGHT BROWN IN COLOUR, THICK DARK OIL

EFFECTS

Feelings of relaxation
and sociability.

Intoxication.
Enhancement of
colours and sounds.

Talkativeness.
Confidence.

Appetite stimulation.

Hallucinations.

PROBLEMS

Paranoia, psychosis
and mood swings.

Tolerance and
habituation.

Cancers of mouth,
throat and chest.

Bronchitis and
emphysema.

Loss of purpose.

Short-term memory
loss.

Changes in ovulation
cycle in females.

Lowered sperm
production in males.

Distortion in time
perception.

SMOKED IN CIGARETTES OR PIPES TAKEN IN FOOD OR DRINKS

POSSESSION ILLEGAL CLASS B DRUG

AMPHETAMINE

COARSE POWDER, USUALLY OFF-WHITE, CAN BE YELLOW OR PINK IN COLOUR, SOMETIMES IN TABLETS OF VARIOUS COLOURS

EFFECTS

Feelings of energy, stamina and strength, euphoria, confidence and exhilaration.

Increase in concentration.

Suppression of appetite.

PROBLEMS

Depression, delusions panic, paranoia and psychosis.

Risk of habituation.

Increase in blood pressure and risk of stroke.

Diarrhoea and increased urination.

Weight loss.

Disturbance of sleep patterns.

Weakened immune system.

Appetite loss.

TAKEN IN DRINKS SWALLOWED IN PAPER 'BOMBS' AND INJECTED

POSSESSION ILLEGAL CLASS B DRUG

COCAINE

WHITE SPARKLING CRYSTALLINE POWDER

EFFECTS

Feelings of energy, stamina and strength, euphoria, confidence and exhilaration.

Increase in concentration.

Loss of inhibitions.

PROBLEMS

Delusions and violent behaviour.

Panic and paranoia.

Tolerance and habituation.

Exhaustion and weight loss.

Weakened immune system.

Damage to nasal passages if snorted.

Collapsed veins or skin ulcers if injected.

'SNORTED' INTO THE NOSE SOMETIMES INJECTED

POSSESSION ILLEGAL CLASS A DRUG

CRACK COCAINE

CRYSTALS OF VARYING SIZES, COLOURS FROM CLEAR TO WHITE OR WITH SHADES OF PINK AND YELLOW

EFFECTS

Extreme feelings of energy, stamina and strength, euphoria, confidence and exhilaration.

Feelings of great mental power.

Feelings of extraordinary physical strength and well-being.

PROBLEMS

Delusions, bizarre and often very violent behaviour.

Panic and paranoia.

Depression, feelings of being under threat.

Tolerance and powerful habituation.

Exhaustion and weight loss.

Weakened immune system.

SMOKED IN SMALL PIPES OR ON FOIL OR BOTTLE TOPS

POSSESSION ILLEGAL CLASS A DRUG

HEROIN

WHITE AND LIGHT TO DARK BROWN POWDERS SOMETIMES IN THE FORM OF WHITE TABLETS

EFFECTS

Feelings of overwhelming euphoria and inner peace.

Complete freedom from anxiety and stress.

Freedom from pain, both mental and physical.

Freedom from hunger and cold.

PROBLEMS

Tolerance and powerful habituation.

Vein collapse and ulceration if injecting.

Damage to immune system.

Loss of body condition and a lowering of general health.

Depressed breathing. Disruption of the menstrual cycle.

Often adulterated with other substances.

Nausea and vomiting.

Severe constipation.

Overdose.

INJECTED INTO VEINS OR SMOKED FROM FOIL

POSSESSION ILLEGAL. CLASS A DRUG

© 1998 David Emmett and Graeme Nice

SOLVENTS

A RANGE OF HOUSEHOLD AND INDUSTRIAL PRODUCTS

EFFECTS

Intense intoxication.

Auditory and visual hallucinations.

Excitability and talkativeness.

Freedom from all cares.

PROBLEMS

Asphyxiation caused by swelling of throat tissues.

Over-stimulation of the heart.

Loss of short-term memory and cognitive skills.

Personality changes.

Accidents whilst intoxicated.

Inhalation of vomit.

Problems with balance.

Problems with speech.

Involuntary urination.

SPRAYED INTO MOUTH OR INHALED FROM BAGS, RAGS OR CONTAINERS

SALE TO UNDER 18-YEAR-OLDS CONTROLLED

ECSTASY

TABLETS AND CAPSULES OF VARIOUS COLOURS AND SHAPES

EFFECTS

Feelings of euphoria, sociability and empathy to others.

Hallucinogenic changes in perception of surroundings.

Energy and stamina.

Increased sexual arousal.

PROBLEMS

Convulsions and sudden death.

Severe overheating and dehydration.

Tolerance and habituation.

Personality changes.

High blood pressure.

Damage to liver and kidneys.

Damage to heart.

Nausea and vomiting.

Mood swings and irritability.

TAKEN BY MOUTH

POSSESSION ILLEGAL CLASS A DRUG

HALLUCINOGENIC MUSHROOMS

SMALL OLIVE-BROWN FUNGI, SEEN FRESH OR DRIED

EFFECTS

Visual and auditory hallucinations.

Feelings of euphoria, high spirits and well being.

Bouts of laughter and giggling.

PROBLEMS

Exposing latent mental problems.

Bouts of dizziness and nausea.

Poisoning as a result of eating the wrong variety.

TAKEN BY MOUTH IN FOOD OR DRINKS

POSSESSION LEGAL IF FRESH, ILLEGAL IF PREPARED FOR USE

NITRITES – POPPERS

SMALL BOTTLES OF CLEAR LIQUID SOLD UNDER VARIOUS BRAND NAMES, LIQUID GOLD, RUSH, STAG ETC.

EFFECTS

Light-headed feelings.

Excitement and exhilaration.

Sexual arousal.

Increased sensitivity of sexual organs.

Relaxes smooth-walled muscles allowing easier anal intercourse.

PROBLEMS

Fainting.

Severe headaches.

Sore eyes.

Damage to sight if allowed to contact eyes.

Nausea and vomiting.

Skin contact rash.

Highly poisonous if swallowed.

INHALED FROM RAGS BAGS OR CONTAINERS

LEGAL (NOT AMYL NITRITE)

ANABOLIC STEROIDS

AMPOULES OF CLEAR LIQUID FOR INJECTION OR AS TABLETS AND CAPSULES OF VARIOUS COLOURS

EFFECTS

Increase in muscle growth and body bulk when used in conjuction with diet and exercise.

Increase in stamina and strength.

PROBLEMS

Mood swings, aggression and irritability.

Tolerance and habituation.

High blood pressure and heart disease.

Liver and kidney cancers.

Liver and kidney dysfunction.

Damage to foetal development.

Shrinking of the testicles, impotence.

Uncontrollable erections.

Bone growth irregularities.

Severe acne.

Disruption of female menstrual cycle.

INJECTED OR BY MOUTH

USE IS LEGAL SUPPLY ONLY BY PRESCRIPTION

TRANQUILLISERS

TABLETS AND CAPSULES OF VARIOUS COLOURS

EFFECTS

Feelings of relaxation euphoria and dreaminess.

Elimination of worry, fear, hunger and cold.

Reduction of withdrawal symptoms from other drugs.

PROBLEMS

Violent mood swings and aggression.

Deep depression.

Bizarre sexual behaviour.

Tolerance, physical and psychological habituation.

Severe withdrawal symptoms.

Lethargy, tiredness, physical weakness and disorientation.

BY MOUTH, TABLETS MAY BE CRUSHED AND INJECTED

POSSESSION ILLEGAL UNLESS UNDER DOCTOR'S PRESCRIPTION CLASS C DRUG

Health Awareness

Suggested age: 15 +

Outline

A multiple format quiz designed to increase participants' awareness of drug-related health issues.

Purpose and expected outcome

- To encourage participants to consider the health implications of drug use.
- To provide accurate information about drugs and health issues.
- To challenge attitudes to drug use.
- To reinforce drug prevention messages.

Method

The quiz comprises 30 questions designed to be suitable for young people aged 15 years and above. Some questions require answers of the true or false variety while others require more detailed answers. They have been produced as three pages of questions. The group leader can decide on the length of the quiz to suit the time available. It should be explained to the participants that the purpose of the quiz is not to examine their level of knowledge about drugs and health issues, but rather to enable them to check out the accuracy of the knowledge that they already have, and to add useful and balanced information. The quiz sheets should be copied and handed out to the participants and time allowed for them to answer the questions. The group leader should then go through the answers using the following guidance notes. Many of the questions will prompt discussion of associated issues.

This is intended and should be encouraged. Participants should correct their answers if necessary and keep the sheets for future reference.

Notes for teacher or group leader

SUGGESTED ANSWERS:

1. **True** – The sharing of injecting equipment can lead to transmission of HIV, hepatitis B and C, and other blood-borne diseases. Drug use can increase libido, lower inhibitions and impair judgement, all of which can lead to users becoming involved in unsafe sex.

2. These drugs have been linked to the following mental health problems:

    Amphetamine (speed) – Depression, paranoia, anxiety, panic attacks, psychosis and schizophrenia.

    Cannabis – Depression, anxiety, paranoia, schizophrenia, psychosis.

    Ecstasy – Depression, anxiety, paranoia, panic attacks, personality disorders.

    LSD (acid) – Anxiety, agitation, panic attacks, personality disorders, flashbacks.

    Cocaine/crack – Panic attacks, depression, paranoia, agitation, aggressive personality disorders.

3. These drugs have been linked to the following physical health problems:

    Amphetamine (speed) – suppressed appetite/weight loss, insomnia, impaired immune system, increased blood pressure, low birth weight and malnourishment in infants.

    Cannabis – breathing disorders, cancers, lowered sperm count/ impotence, low birth weight in infants, higher mortality in infants.

    Ecstasy – overheating, dehydration, impaired kidney and liver function, damage to brain cells, facial muscle spasm, convulsions.

    Cocaine/crack – damage to nasal tissues if snorted, increased blood pressure, exhaustion, nausea, respiratory problems if smoked, infants born withdrawing from drug.

    Heroin – Indifference to pain, suppressed appetite, impotence, constipation, physical addiction and withdrawal, various extra dangers if injected (see note below).

    Magic mushrooms – risk of poisoning, vomiting, diarrhoea.

NB: If any drug is used intravenously this brings additional problems and risks, such as vein collapse, abscess, blood poisoning, gangrene, infections.

4. **True** – Used in the past to relieve the symptoms of angina and to revive people who had fainted (liquid smelling salts).

5. The higher blood pressure in an artery may prevent injection and can lead to excessive blood loss. Drugs are commonly injected into veins rather than into muscle or arteries because the vein carries blood directly back to the heart for distribution throughout the body. Injecting a drug also produces a much quicker and more intense response than when taken orally.

6. **True** – Research suggests that the high tar content of cannabis, high burning temperature, and greater number of recognised cancerous agents in its smoke pose a greater risk of cancer than tobacco use alone.

7. **True** – The most commonly used mushroom, the liberty cap, is easily confused with many other varieties, some of which are poisonous. If dried, correct identification is almost impossible.

8. LSD is the most powerful psychoactive drug known. Experiences may be negative or positive, and the adverse side effects can include hallucinations, flashbacks, panic, paranoia, reality distortion, increased accident risk whilst hallucinating, and possible long-term mental illness.

9. All answers are correct, depending on degree and length of use, and the testing process used. For example, regular use may be detected in the urine for up to 30 days, whereas testing of human hair may indicate cannabis use for a much longer period.

10. Amphetamine (speed) suppresses appetite and increases metabolism. This can lead to malnutrition of the mother and her foetus, resulting in low birth weight and the risk of physical or mental damage to the unborn child.

11. All legal and illegal drugs that enter the mother's bloodstream, whether smoked, injected, snorted or taken orally, have the potential to cross the placental barrier and adversely affect the foetus.

12. Anabolic steroid use by males can lead to:

    - reduced testicle size (irreversible);
    - aggression (roid rage), possibly of a sexual nature;
    - acne;
    - irregular bone growth (especially in adolescents);
    - liver and kidney cancer;
    - raised blood pressure;

- water retention;

- lowered sperm output;

- over-development of breasts (can be irreversible).

13. Anabolic steroid use by females can lead to:

- enlargement of the clitoris;

- deepening voice;

- growth of facial and body hair;

- male pattern baldness;

- decrease in breast size;

- disruption of menstrual cycle;

- damage to foetus during preganancy.

14. **Physical addiction** – The need to repeatedly use a drug in order to avoid physical withdrawal symptoms, such as stomach cramps, aching joints, 'flu like symptoms, insomnia, tremors, etc.

    Psychological addiction – The psychological need to repeatedly use a drug due to feelings of being unable to cope without it. These feelings are usually unfounded, but can be powerful.

15. **Tolerance** – The need to use ever increasing amounts of a drug in order to obtain the desired effects. Tolerance will build with regular use of a drug, but will quickly fade once use has ceased.

16. **20 minutes** – The short duration of effects can lead to repeated use of cocaine.

17. **All are correct** – The duration of the hallucinatory trip can vary widely, and depends on factors such as tolerance, mood of user, environment, expectations of user, etc.

18. Street drugs that are found in powder or tablet form are generally adulterated with substances to increase weight and bulk and therefore profit margins to the supplier. Many of these extra substances are of a harmless nature, whilst others can place the user at some risk, especially if the drug is being injected. Examples of dangerous impurities include brick dust or chalk which can clog small blood vessels, poisonous substances such as strychnine, or other drugs which may cause an adverse effect to that expected.

19. **Brain** – Tissue damage and impairment of neurotransmitter action can occur. Overheating caused by the drug can lead to cerebral convulsions and death.

    Kidney – Impairs function of this organ which can result in water retention. Also linked to kidney cancer.

    Jaws – Can cause spasm of facial muscles, leading to a form of lockjaw.

Heart – Increases heart rate and therefore blood pressure which can be dangerous for those with cardiac weakness.

Lungs – Is linked with pulmonary embolisms (blood clots), which can lead to death.

20. **Dehydration** can result from overheating caused by ecstasy use which induces heavy perspiration. Dehydration can lead to severe cramps, excess levels of salts in the blood, over concentration of urine, fainting and collapse. Users of the drug must therefore replace this lost fluid. The current advice is to sip a pint of water each hour, preferably in the form of an isotonic drink.

21. **The adrenal gland** – This results in the over-production of the hormone adrenaline, which can lead to increased and irregular heart rate and panic attacks. In extreme cases this can result in cardiac arrest and death.

22. The combined effects of two similar types of drug, such as ecstasy and amphetamine (stimulants) or heroin and alcohol (depressants), can lead to life-threatening situations. Two depressant drugs used together can slow the body's functions to standstill and death. On the other hand, two stimulant drugs used together can lead to over-stimulation, overheating, strain on the heart and brain and, again, eventual death. The mixing of dissimilar drugs can lead to unpredictable and potentially dangerous effects.

23. Withdrawal symptoms from heroin include:

    - diarrhoea – leading to dehydration and cramps;

    - aching joints and runny nose;

    - insomnia;

    - fluctuations in skin temperature;

    - headaches;

    - tremors;

    - sweating;

    - muscle spasms.

24. Check ABC.

    - Airway – check that airway is open and unobstructed.

    - Breathing – check that the friend is breathing.

    - Circulation – check for pulse or heart beat.

    - Move the friend to a safe environment if possible and necessary.

    - Place in recovery position.

- Check temperature: if he/she is hot then attempt to cool; if cold then cover to keep warm.

- Reassure by talking, even if you think the friend is unconscious.

- Summon help by telephoning 999 to ambulance service.

- Stay with the friend until the arrival of medical help.

- Keep any evidence of the substance used and hand it to medical staff.

25. **True** – Literally, 'what goes up must come down'. Stimulant use produces feelings of being 'high' which is always followed by a corresponding 'low', leading in many cases to depression.

26. Depression – **True.**

    Withdrawal – **True.**

    Obesity – **False.**

    Acne – **False.**

    Insomnia – **True.**

    Aggression – **True.**

    Irregular heart beat – **True.**

    Sterility – **False.**

    Diarrhoea – **False.**

27. **Hyperthermia (overheating)** – Ecstasy, amphetamine.

    Weight loss – Amphetamine, cocaine.

    Cancer – Cannabis, ecstasy, anabolic steroids.

    Paranoia – Cannabis, amphetamine, LSD, ecstasy, cocaine.

    Asphyxia – Solvents.

    Overdose – Heroin, cocaine, amphetamine.

28. The use of certain drugs can lead to an increased libido, a reduction in inhibitions and a loss of judgement and control. This may then place the users in situations where unsafe sex may follow.

29. Both cannabis and steroid use can affect male fertility by reducing the levels of certain hormones and therefore sperm production and motility. The menstrual cycle in women can be adversely affected by the use of cannabis, ecstasy, steroids or heroin.

30. (a) **True** – Can be used to ward off the withdrawal effects of some illegal drugs, may be misused in their own right for their effects, or overused by those who have been prescribed them. Overuse can be as a result of tolerance or the need for an emotional or chemical prop.

    (b) **True** – Many pharmaceutical substances, especially those in tablet, capsule or powder form, can be sold under the guise of other street substances, such as ecstasy, amphetamine, heroin and cocaine.

(c) **True** – Many pharmaceutical drugs are prescribed for short term use only. Extended periods of use can lead to both physical and psychological addiction. Abrupt withdrawal from some of these substances can be very dangerous.

Follow-up exercises

The quiz will have raised many health issues connected with drug use. Any of these can be followed up with discussions, research projects, essay writing or in any other way that the group leader sees as being appropriate and useful.

HEALTH AWARENESS

1. Drug use can lead to HIV infection.   **True/False**

2. Which illegal drugs can lead to mental health problems?

   ....

3. Which illegal drugs can lead to physical health problems ?

   ....

4. Poppers (nitrites) have been used for medical purposes.   **True/False**

5. Drugs are commonly injected into veins. Why is this?

   ....

6. Cannabis smoking carries a high cancer risk. **True/False**

7. Magic mushrooms can be easily confused with other, more poisonous, varieties.   **True/False**

8. What are the possible side effects of LSD use?

9. Cannabis can be detected in the human body for? **2 days / 1 week /1 month / 6 months /2 years**

10. If pregnant women use amphetamine (speed), how can this affect their unborn chid?

11. Which other drugs can affect unborn infants if their mothers use them?

    ....

12. What side effects can occur in men who use anabolic steroids?

    ....

HEALTH AWARENESS

13. What side effects can occur in women who use anabolic steroids?

   ....

14. Explain the difference between physical and psychological addiction.

   ....

15. Repeated ecstasy use can lead to tolerance. What does this mean?

   ....

16. The desired effects of cocaine usually last for?
   20 mins/2 hours/6 hours/12 hours

17. An LSD trip, whether good or bad, can last for how long?
   3 hours/15 mins/10 hours/24 hours/45 mins

18. How can the impurities commonly found in street drugs affect the users health?

   ....

19. Ecstasy use can have a bad effect on which parts of the body?
   Brain/Kidney/Jaws/Heart/Lungs

20. Why is dehydration a problem for ecstasy users?

   ....

21. Which gland is stimulated by solvent use, and how does this affect the body?

   ....

22. Why can mixing drugs be especially dangerous?

   ....

23. List the physical withdrawal symptoms from heroin.

   ....

HEALTH AWARENESS

24. If a friend collapses after using drugs, what steps can you take to help?

....

25. The use of a stimulant drug, such as speed and cocaine, can leave you feeling depressed. **True/False**

26. The caffeine content of some soft drinks can lead to which of the following health problems?

    **Depression/Withdrawal/Obesity/Acne/Insomnia/
    Aggression/Irregular heartbeat/Sterility/Diarrhoea**

27. The following health problems are associated with which drug or drugs?
    **Overheating/Weight loss/Cancer/Paranoia/
    Asphyxia/Overdose**

    ....

28. What are the links between drug use and unsafe sexual practices?

    ....

29. Which drugs affect fertility in males, and menstruation in females?

    ....

30. Some prescribed drugs can be:
    (a) misused; **True/False**
    (b) sold as other drugs; **True/False**
    (c) addictive. **True/False**

EXERCISE 16

Just Another Ordinary Day

Suggested age: 13 +

Outline

An exercise that uses a short but eventful story to promote discussion of a number of potentially dangerous drug-related incidents.

Purpose and expected outcome

- To increase the participants' sense of community responsibility.
- To encourage individual responsibility over drug decisions.
- To see personal drug use in a wider context.
- To challenge attitudes to drug use.
- To reinforce drug prevention messages.

Method

The group leader should outline the exercise to the class and then split them up into small groups. Copies of the story are then distributed to each group and participants should be asked to read it and consider the various situations that Mary encounters. The groups should list each incident and the hazards that are apparent. They should also consider what actions Mary might have taken in each case, and what her alternative decisions are at each point. After sufficient time has been allowed, the groups should be asked to report back to the class as a whole the results of their considerations. The rest of the class should be encouraged to comment upon the points being raised. It may be necessary for the leader to restrict each group's report to a particular incident or a small number of incidents in order that each group has the opportunity to make their report.

When each of the groups has made their reports, the leader should briefly draw together the points made by the class and the lessons that have come out of the exercise.

As an alternative the story can be read by the leader to the class as a whole, and points raised by individual class members and then discussed.

Notes for teacher or group leader

Mary's life is deliberately brimming with drug-related incidents. It is not intended to represent any sort of typical day, but offers differing sorts of incidents that people may have to face in real life.

Follow-up exercises

The story would make an excellent basis for some imaginative role-play work or could be used as a stimulus for written work, for example, a newspaper report on local drug use.

Just Another Ordinary Day

Mary Brown was having a bad day. The washing machine had broken and her baby, Rebecca, had been awake throughout the night. Mary reached for the paracetamol, and initially took two; but then took a further two as she had a splitting headache. She then placed the open bottle on the coffee table near to where Rebecca was playing.

About half an hour later, Mary decided to venture out to the shops with Rebecca, taking the short-cut across the park. Rebecca ran on ahead, and started to play with some items she found in a flower bed. Mary was horrified to find that Rebecca had found some discarded needles and syringes, and immediately took them and placed them into a wastepaper bin nearby.

Over by the bandstand a boy was acting in a drunken manner. He dropped what looked like an aerosol can, and staggered off in the direction of the bridge by the canal that ran alongside the park. Mary knew the boy – he was Ronnie, a neighbour's son – but she decided not to tell the boy's mother as she did not want to get him into any trouble.

On reaching the shops Mary met her friend Dennis, and they talked for a while as they watched a group of young people who were drinking in a nearby bus shelter. As they watched, two of the group rode off at speed on a motorcycle towards the motorway and the rest of the group then walked off, leaving behind a girl who appeared to be asleep on her back in the bus shelter. Mary and Dennis shrugged their shoulders at what they saw, but decided that this is how young people are today and that it was nothing to do with them.

Mary told Dennis about how awful she felt and how tired she was. Dennis offered to get her something he bought from a friend of his which he said would give her energy and lift her depression. Mary was grateful for this offer, and handed over £10 to pay for it. She asked Dennis if he was sure that it would be good for her. Dennis took the money and reassured her.

Once Mary had all of her shopping, she decided to catch a bus over to her mother's house on the other side of town. There they ate a meal, and Mary tried to settle Rebecca down for a nap, but the child was irritable and restless. Mary's mother suggested that they give her half of one of the sleeping pills prescribed by her doctor, but Rebecca would not swallow it.

Just Another Ordinary Day

Later that evening, Mary asked if her mother would babysit, as she wanted to go out clubbing with some of her friends. The club she went to was the Seventh Heaven at the end of the high street. It became increasingly hot inside as the dance floor began to fill up, and Mary had a couple of vodka and tonics to cool off. Later on, one of her friends came back with some tablets he had just bought and suggested that they all take one to have a good time. Mary was a little unsure, but took one anyway as she didn't want to be left out. She carried on dancing but began to feel hot and dizzy. She went to the toilet and quickly collapsed in one of the cubicles. When she had not returned after 20 minutes, one of her friends went to look for her, and found her lying unconscious.

An ambulance was called and Mary was taken to hospital. None of her friends mentioned what she had taken to the ambulance crew, as they did not want to get her into any trouble.

After a few days, however, Mary was beginning to recover when she was visited by one of her neighbours, who asked her how all this had happened. Mary replied that she couldn't remember, but in any case it wasn't her fault she was sure.

Six Things to Consider

Suggested age: 14 +

Outline

A didactic exercise aimed at young people who may have tried drugs, been offered them, or who may soon be placed in a situation where they have to make a decision about them.

Purpose and expected outcome

- To improve the level of young peoples' knowledge about drugs.
- To encourage responsibility for personal decisions about drugs and their use.
- To reduce the harm caused by certain forms of drug taking.
- To challenge attitudes to drug use.
- To reinforce drug prevention messages.

Method

The worksheet shows the six major issues that those who are using drugs may have to face up to. This sheet can be used as an OHP or copied and distributed to the class members as an *aide memoire,* or for them to add notes to, during the lesson. The accompanying teachers notes explain how some of these issues are linked, outlining the dangers and problems associated with each.

The teacher or group leader should outline the purpose of the exercise to the members of class, and then work through the accompanying notes with them. The class can be encouraged to discuss and comment upon each section of the notes as it is worked through.

At the end of the exercise the leader should draw together the main points that have come out of the discussions.

Notes for teacher or group leader

TOLERANCE

Tolerance to any drug will build rapidly if the drug is used on a regular basis. In order to get the same effect as that achieved initially, greater quantities of the drug must be used on each subsequent occasion. This is because the body becomes accustomed to its use and effects, and tries to even these out by changing its reaction to them. Tolerance will build with the use of illegal street drugs, legal drugs such as alcohol, nicotine and coffee, and even some medical drugs, if used for a long enough period. Tolerance will fade once use of the drug has ceased.

COST

Once tolerance to a specific drug begins to build, it will necessitate the user buying or obtaining ever greater amounts of the drug to get the desired effect. This is great news to the dealer or supplier, as he or she will become more in demand as clients have to buy more and more drugs. On the other hand, the cost to the individual user will only increase, whereas the effects from the use of greater amounts will remain much as before. Increased drug use drives many users to steal, borrow or beg what they need, whilst countless others will turn to prostitution or other serious forms of crime to feed habits, which for some users can reach anything up to £200 per day. Even heavy cannabis users can find themselves needing as much as £150 per week. Many drug users will be forced to sell possessions to which they may be very attached, to realise only a fraction of their true value.

ADDICTION

Drug users may become physically or psychologically addicted to substances they use. If use of the preferred drug is stopped or reduced once a tolerance has built, due to non-availability or expense, then users will begin to feel unpleasant symptoms of physical or psychological withdrawal. These may lead to great pain or discomfort and sufferers may feel that they cannot carry on with their normal day to day lives without use of the drug. Many heavy users of drugs no longer get any positive feelings from the drugs that they use, but may simply take them to feel 'normal'. Many drug addicts will then turn to injecting drugs to achieve greater effects.

WITHDRAWAL

Withdrawal symptoms from drug use can range from slight discomfort to life-threatening situations, depending on the drug or drugs being used, their strength and purity, the quantities used and the regularity of use. Withdrawal symptoms are common with illegal drugs and some legal drugs too, such as alcohol (hangover), nicotine (cravings and mood changes) and even coffee (anxiety). In certain circumstances withdrawal symptoms can necessitate hospitalisation. Medical supervision, advice and intervention is recommended for all serious situations. Abrupt withdrawal from some drugs, such as heroin or even tranquillisers, can lead to death.

HEALTH

All substances that are taken into the body, either by mouth, injection, smoking or sniffing, eventually find their way to the brain via the bloodstream. They will be filtered and processed by the lungs, stomach, liver and kidneys. Apart from the fact that brain cells may be killed off (e.g. with alcohol or ecstasy use), use of drugs cause many other health related problems as follows:

HEROIN

Overdose (due to depressant effect), physical addiction, withdrawal symptoms that could be life threatening. HIV, hepatitis, gangrene, collapsed veins, septicaemia, abscesses due to injecting, etc.

AMPHETAMINE (SPEED)

Mental illness, psychosis, paranoia, depression, anxiety, immune system damage leading to other illnesses, hyperthermia (overheating), insomnia, etc.

ECSTASY

Blood clots, hyperthermia, confusion, lockjaw, dehydration, kidney and liver cancer, brain damage, personality disorders, etc.

CANNABIS

Short-term memory loss; loss of co-ordination; cancers of tongue, lips, throat, mouth and lungs; bronchitis; impotency; psychosis; paranoia; schizophrenia; etc.

ALCOHOL

Cirrhosis of liver, death of brain cells, loss of co-ordination, raised blood pressure, death if used with certain other depressant drugs, mental illnesses, personality disorders.

INJECTING

Hepatitis B or C virus, which could lead to serious or fatal health problems in later life; HIV; gangrene; collapsed veins; septicaemia; abscesses; etc.

ADULTERANTS

The majority of street drugs are also 'cut' or adulterated with other substances that are potentially harmful, especially if injected. It is quite common for substances to be sold that are not what they claim to be at all. These are known as 'snidey' drugs and can contain all sorts of dangerous substances.

ILLEGALITY

The majority of street drugs are illegal substances and the possession of them can lead to a court conviction and a prison sentence. Manufacture or supply of an illegal drug can attract even greater sentences and the offenders assets may also be seized. In law the offence of 'supplying' is complete if a person simply passes a 'joint' or 'spliff' to another person for them to take a draw from. No money needs to change hands.

Once a person has a drugs conviction, it can stay with them for life and cause all sorts of problems, such as restrictions in career choices and travel opportunities. Many professions, businesses, etc. will not take on a person with a drugs conviction, and many countries throughout the world will not grant entry visas to them for the same reason.

It is not true that the police only caution for possession of drugs nowadays, it depends upon many other circumstances, such as class of drug and amount.

Drugs are classified into three groups depending on how dangerous they are considered to be.

CLASS A – Heroin, cocaine, crack, ecstasy, LSD.

CLASS B – Cannabis, amphetamine.

CLASS C – Mostly prescription tranquillisers and hypnotics.

For penalties, see the worksheet for this chapter.

Follow-up exercises

The exercise can be supported and reinforced by the distribution to participants of drug information literature for them to study in their own time.

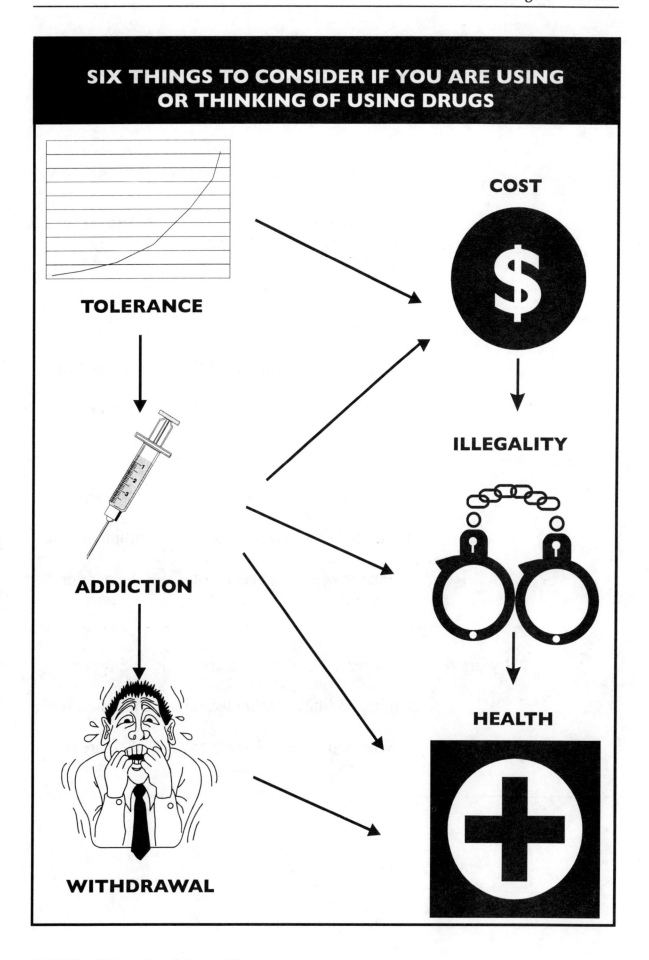

PENALTIES

	Possession for own use	Possession with intent to supply	Supply	Manufacture or cultivation
A	7 years	Life Unlimited fine Seizure of assets	Life Unlimited fine Seizure of assets	Life Unlimited fine Seizure of assets
B	5 years	14 years Unlimited fine Seizure of assets	14 years Unlimited fine Seizure of assets	14 years Unlimited fine Seizure of assets
C	2 years	5 years Unlimited fine Seizure of assets	5 years Unlimited fine Seizure of assets	5 years Unlimited fine Seizure of assets

An Unnecessary Death

Suggested age: 13 +

Outline

An exercise that can be used as a stimulus for discussion work, role-play and writing. It allows participants to explore several aspects that surround the accidental death of a young person who is under the influence of lighter fuel gas, and the actions of his friends.

Purpose and expected outcome

- To encourage participants to consider the possible results of substance use in dangerous circumstances.
- To allow participants to examine the responsibilities of a drug user's friends.
- To enable participants to consider the wider consequences of individual drug use.
- To challenge attitudes to drug use.
- To reinforce drug prevention messages.

Method

Using the story worksheet as a stimulus, the class can be set all or some of the following tasks.

TASK ONE

Write a dramatic essay about the accident and the circumstances leading up to it. You may invent any fact or other characters that you wish to include, you but must not change any of the given facts. Make the essay as dramatic as possible.

TASK TWO

Working in pairs, one person to take the part of a police officer and the other person the part of a witness to the accident. The police officer is to interview the witness about what he/she saw and prepare a written statement based on that interview. The pair can then swap round so that they change roles. A specimen police statement form is included for this task.

TASK THREE

Such an accident would certainly make the front page of your local newspaper. Reproduce that front page, including the masthead, headline and feature story, together with any other extras that might be found on the front page of your local newspaper. The story should be written in a journalistic style and include at least one short quote from a witness.

TASK FOUR

Write a letter to your local newspaper expressing your views about the accident. The letter is for publication and should be powerful and to the point.

TASK FIVE

Write a letter from one of the group of friends to John's parents. The letter should express how sorry you are about what happened. The letter need not be overlong but should convey in a clear way exactly how you feel.

Role-plays

The story can also be used as a stimulus for individuals or groups to role-play the following situations:

1. The conversation between John and the rest of the group when he suggests to them that they should buy some gas and use it by the railway line.

2. The decision of Paul and Liza not to use gas on that day and the reaction of the rest of the group to that decision.

3. The time that Helen and John told the rest of the group about their use of amphetamine and the reaction of the rest of the group to the information.

4. The actions of Paul and Liza whilst the other members of the group are sniffing, and their conversations.

5. The moment when Jason reaches John's dead body just after it has been struck by the train.

6. The moment when the train driver reaches the body after bringing the train to an emergency stop.

7. The rest of the group's reaction to the accident in the first few minutes following the collision.

8. The arrival of the police and their conversations with the group members.

9. The arrival of the police at John's home and their conversation with his parents, telling them of the accident.

10. The moment when John's parents tell his brothers and sisters about the accident, and their reactions to the news.

11. A conversation between John's mother and the rest of the group some days after the accident, during which she blames them for what happened.

12. A conversation between the train driver and other rail workers concerning nightmares about seeing John right in front of the train cab just before the impact.

13. A conversation between the surviving members of the group after attending John's funeral.

14. A conversation between John's parents following the funeral.

15. An assembly given by the head teacher of John's school, telling the rest of the school about the accident at the start of the new term. This will include the head's thoughts about the responsibilities of all concerned.

Notes for teacher or group leader

The written part of this exercise can form the basis of a number of lessons, spaced out over several weeks. The role play part of the exercise can be carried out in small groups or using the whole class. The whole story can be used as a basis for a complete dramatic play about the incident which could then be performed in front of the whole school or indeed taken to other schools in the area.

Follow-up exercises

An accidental death of this nature would be the subject of a legal inquest of some sort. The story could be used as the basis for holding a mock inquest into all of the circumstances surrounding the accident. At such an inquest each member of the group would be required to attend and give evidence along with anyone else involved in the accident, during which they would be questioned by lawyers representing the rail authorities and by the coroner.

AN UNNECESSARY DEATH

The main railway line ran in a shallow cutting along the back of the allotments near to the Manor's Field housing estate. The time was 11.45 am on Monday 15 August. Five youths, John Weston, Jason Fielding, Liza Williams, Paul Shields and Helen Roberts, all 14-year-olds, were sitting at the foot of the embankment close to the line.

The members of the group were on holiday from school and this was a favourite place for them to meet. The railway line was fenced off, but a part of the fence had been broken down earlier that summer and the friends had no difficulty in getting through. They liked the place because it was out of the sight of anyone working on the allotments. They occupied their time exploring the copse at the edge of the line and messing about in the small work huts that lay close to the line. Trains passed about every 20 minutes, and the members of the group had hidden from them at first because they feared that the driver would report them to the police for trespassing, but after the first few times they had got fed up with hiding and now didn't bother whether they were seen or not.

On this particular day the friends moved into one of the work huts, some of them sniffing lighter fuel gas from refill canisters: they had all tried gas several times before, and all had smoked cannabis on lots of occasions. John and Helen had told the others that they had also tried amphetamine and ecstasy. On this particular day it had been John's idea to buy some cans of gas from one of the local shops, and to use it by the railway line. Liza and Paul had decided not to sniff on that day but the others used the gas for a few minutes and, with the exception of Helen were all shouting and laughing and getting very high. Helen had been very sick and had passed out on the floor in the corner of the hut. John did not like the sight or smell of the vomit and staggered outside. He sat for a few minutes until his can of gas was empty, and then he began to pick up stones from the side of the line. At first he just threw the stones randomly all around him, but then he began to throw them through the smashed windows of the hut at the rest of the group. He was laughing hysterically as he did so, and fell over several times.

AN UNNECESSARY DEATH

One of the stones hit Jason on the forehead, after bouncing off an inside wall, and made a deep cut. Jason got very angry and ran out of the hut screaming and shouting at the top of his voice. He was completely out of control and picked up a heavy piece of metal. John laughed at him and threw another stone. This missed Jason, and he chased John along the edge of the track. They had only gone a few yards when Jason was passed by a fast-moving Inter City train travelling along the line nearest to him. John had his back to the train and was so high on the gas that he didn't hear it coming. He turned to run across the tracks and was struck by the train. The impact threw him half-way up the embankment. He suffered massive injuries all over his body and died instantly.

STATEMENT FORM

Witness Statement

Statement of: . . . .

Age if under 21: . . . .   (if over 21 insert 'over 21')

This statement (consisting of . . . . pages each signed by me) is true to the best of my knowledge and belief and I make it knowing that, if it is tendered in evidence, I shall be liable to prosecution if I have willfully stated in it anything which I know to be false or do not believe to be true.

Date: . . . . day of . . . . 19/20 . . . .

Signature: . . . .

. . . .

. . . .

. . . .

. . . .

. . . .

. . . .

. . . .

. . . .

. . . .

. . . .

. . . .

. . . .

. . . .

. . . .

. . . .

. . . .

Signature: . . . .

Signature witnessed by:. . . . .

National Helping Agencies in the UK

National Drugs Help Line
Tel. 0800 77 66 00
Website http://drugs.hea.org.uk
(Free, confidential 24-hour service to users, their families and friends)

RE-SOLV
30a High Street, Stone, Staffordshire ST15 8AW
Tel. 01785 817885
(Works to reduce and prevent solvent abuse)

SCODA – Standing Conference on Drug Abuse
32–36 Loman Street, London SE1 0EE
Tel. 0171-928 9500
(National co-ordinating body for agencies and organisations working in the drugs field)

Release
388 Old Street, London EC1V 8LT
Tel. 0171-729 9904 or 0171-603 8654
(24-hour advice, information and referral on legal and drug-related problems for users, their families and friends)

National AIDS Helpline
Tel. 0800 567 123
(24-hour advice and counselling service)

Welsh Committee on Drug Misuse
Secretariat, c/o HSSPIA, Welsh Office, Cathays Park, Cardiff CF1 3NQ
Tel. 01222 823925
(Details of local services and literature on substance misuse)

Scottish Drugs Forum
5 Waterloo Street, Glasgow G2 6AY
Tel. 0141-221 1175
(Details of drug services in Scotland)

Northern Ireland Council for Voluntary Action
127 Ormeau Road, Belfast BT7 1SH
Tel. 01232 321224
(Details of drug services in Northern Ireland)

Samaritans
National Lo-call number 0345 90 90 90
For local branches consult your telephone directory

Alcoholics Anonymous
National Lo-call number 0345 697555

Citizens Advice Bureau
For local branches consult your telephone directory

Childline
0800 11 11
(For children in trouble or danger)

For details of other voluntary and statutory agencies in your area that may be able to offer help, advice or information, look in your local telephone directory under 'help and advice'.